THE POWER
OF ART AND NATURE

10 Ways Both Can Improve Your Life

Tammy Mitzka-Crawford

10-10-10
Publishing

THE POWER OF ART AND NATURE:
Ten Ways Both Can Improve Your Life
www.powerofartandnature.com
Copyright © 2022 Tammy Mitzka-Crawford

Paperback ISBN: 979-8-355491-15-4

References to internet websites (URLs) were accurate at the time of writing. Authors and the publishers are not responsible for URLs that may have expired or changed since the manuscript was prepared.

Limits of Liability and Disclaimer of Warranty
The author and publisher shall not be liable for your misuse of the enclosed material. This book is strictly for informational and educational purposes only.

Warning – Disclaimer
The purpose of this book is to educate and entertain. The author and/or publisher do not guarantee that anyone following these techniques, suggestions, tips, ideas, or strategies will become successful. The author and/or publisher shall have neither liability nor responsibility to anyone with respect to any loss or damage caused, or alleged to be caused, directly or indirectly by the information contained in this book.

Publisher
10-10-10 Publishing
Markham, ON Canada

Printed in Canada and the United States of America

Table of Contents

Dedication v

Testimonials vii

About the Author...ix

Acknowledgements xi

Foreword...xxi

Chapter 1: Live 1

Chapter 2: Change...15

Chapter 3: Inspiration..31

Chapter 4: Uniqueness 53

Chapter 5: Creativeness 69

Chapter 6: Time...87

Chapter 7: Positivity 99

Chapter 8: Fun...113

Chapter 9: Communication 129

Chapter 10: Lifestyle..141

Dedication

This book is dedicated to the dreamers, the risk-takers, and the trailblazers who have taken the road less traveled. It is for those who have dared to forge their own path, even when it means going against the grain.

It is for those who have dedicated their lives to following their passion, even when it wasn't the easy thing to do. This book is for you. You are the ones who have shown us that anything is possible if you believe in yourself and are willing to work hard.

It can be hard to follow our hearts in a world that often tells us to conform. The safe path is well-lit and well-marked, but it doesn't always lead to where we want to go. So, for everyone who has ever taken the road less traveled, this book is for you.

Whether an entrepreneur chasing your dreams or an artist following your vision, you are blazing a new trail. And that takes courage. So, keep going. Keep exploring. And never let anyone tell you that you cannot achieve your goals. You have the power to create your own destiny. So go out there and make something great. Thank you for inspiring us to chase our dreams and follow our hearts.

Testimonials

"Tammy continuously inspires others to fully embrace life's challenges with a sense of lightness and hope. She unlocks and shares serenity through her art in a captivating manner. Tammy's story will not only deeply touch your heart, but it also gives you tangible insights into the power of healing through art and nature."
Jessica Shelley, Serial Entrepreneur and Partner at Industry Rockstar®

"Tammy eloquently weaves together her life, as she does the story telling in this book. Her innate ability to connect with people and intuitive skills is seamlessly executed. Tammy maintains a high vibrational experience around positivity. Her book teaches the system that connects the beauty of art with the glorious outcomes of life."
KORIE MINKUS
CEO & Founder, Rock Your Product®
The #1 Global Product Business Advisory & Growth Training Company, #1 Bestselling Author

About the Author

Tammy Crawford is an internationally published author and speaker. She is also internation-ally known for her inspirational fine art and 3-D wall sculptures, reliefs, murals, and paintings. Her unique originals sell from 5 to 6 figures.

Tammy started selling art at 14, has taken on various art projects, and has taught art privately and publicly. Her artwork has been featured and published in multiple media outlets, including magazines, newspapers, and television.

Tammy's dedication to philanthropy has included raising funds for children's charities, mentoring, and art education. Originally from Oregon, she now lives in beautiful North Idaho, surrounded by trees, lakes, wildlife, and peace.

Her mission: To enhance people's lives by creating beautiful art that causes them to reflect, imagine, and be inspired.

To check out Tammy's art: mitzkafinearts.com
Book website: powerofartandnature.com
Social media: Mitzkafinearts, powerofartandnature, or Tammy
Mitzka-Crawford
Questions: powerofartandnature.com

Acknowledgements

I want to start by thanking **God**. I am truly grateful for all the blessings in my life. Without **His** love, protection, and guidance, I would not be here today. **God** has been my biggest inspiration in life. I look outside and see all the beauty that he has created, and I am in awe. The world is so vast; there is so much to explore.

I am thankful for my wonderful husband, **Darryl Crawford**. He is the one person who truly understands me. He is my best friend and inspires me to be a better person. I know that no matter what challenges we face, we can overcome them as long as we are together.

My family: **Chelsey & Jed, Brandi & Joey**, and our five amazing grandchildren, **Ethan, Gavin, Noah, Violett**, and **Nataylia**. They are my whole world and remind me of the importance of living in the present and being grateful for what I have.

To **Jesse & Melanee Micka, Jeff & Brenda Micka, Angie & Craig Shantie, Mike & Tammy Crawford**, and all my nieces and nephews, you are all so special to me, and I cherish our shared moments.

I am grateful for each of these ladies. They are the ones who make me laugh when I am feeling down and who help me to see the silver lining in every cloud—lending a listening ear when I need to talk and always ready to offer a helping hand when needed. Thank you for your support, your laughter, and your love. Thank you for being you: **Philomina Bender, Pam Garland, Melissa Couch, Lissa Mina, Maria Janete McNall, & Brenette Leifer**

I am grateful for the continued support of **all** my professional acquaintances, friends, and devoted fans. You continually inspire and encourage me with your kind words and affirmations! Thank you from the bottom of my heart. A few of my top advocates: **Jang Pimvisat, Lori Beard, Mary Beth Buchanan, Cindy Goff, Conrad Bagley, Evelyn Wong, KLS Fuerte, Janet Spangler, Dawn Fowler, Janice D'Aloia, Heidi Riley, Rayna Hahn, Cindy Nana, Margaret Brock, Sherry McFarland, Eike Capelle, Trish Toohey, Manda Wycliff, Alex Quinones, Sandra Reynolds, Ase Elvebakk, Tulasi Ilen, Eunice Ifeanyichukwu, Riley Haun, and Andreas John**.

I am so grateful that my clients (many of whom prefer to remain anonymous) have chosen me to be their artist. It is such an honor to be able to create one-of-a-kind masterpieces that will be cherished for generations. I am inspired by their stories and treasure the friendships we have made.

Some of my treasured clients include:

Sonja & David, thank you for letting me create "Golden Eagle Falls" for your beautiful entryway and for purchasing "Stillness in the Reeds."

Sheree & Casey Bryntesen (Ironstone Furniture & Fire), thank you for purchasing many of my art pieces and continuing to showcase my art.

Brenette & Ed Leifer (Blades Design Group), thank you for being one of the first to believe in me, always supporting me, and letting me create two beautiful mystical wall sculptures for you & your salon.

Chuck and Julie Miller, thanks for hiring me to create an original, unique wall sculpture, "Dreaming Idaho," that reminds you of why you love Idaho. Thank you for always sharing and showing your support!

Keith Boe, thanks for hiring me to create a large aspen tree to use as a power source for the restaurant and sharing in North Idaho Life.

Pam & Greg Garland, thanks for purchasing "Chosen" and for your constant encouragement, support, and everything you do.

My coaches, mentors, and those who have inspired me:

Thank you, **Korie Minkus Trevino**, for being a fantastic business advisor/coach and friend! You always listen, encourage, inspire, and share your knowledge with me. I am grateful for your friendship and your support.

Thank you, **Jessica Shelley**, for always taking the time to listen to me and providing excellent advice. You always come up with brilliant ideas to keep me motivated and moving forward. Your coaching and friendship are a blessing to me.

Alessia Minkus, you are a great role model and set a high standard for me and others to follow. Your coaching inspires others to be their best and reach their potential. I appreciate your support and friendship. Thank you.

Kane Minkus, thank you for being an amazing coach! I always look forward to your classes and group coaching calls because you always make me laugh. You have a way of making people feel comfortable, inspiring them to be creative and take action. Thank you for everything!

Thank you, **Les Brown,** for inspiring me to tell my story. Your examples of great storytelling have shown me that it is possible to overcome any obstacle if I set my mind to it. Your stories have also inspired me to be creative in how I tell my own stories.

Kevin Harrington, you are a true inspiration, not just for entrepreneurs but for anyone who wants to follow their dreams and make a difference in the world. You have a unique perspective and approach to business. I admire your creativity and your ability to see opportunities in a different way.

Thank you, **Lisa Vrancken,** for being the amazing woman that you are. Your encouragement and support have meant the world to me. I am truly grateful for your friendship, and I know we will continue to support each other in the future. Thanks again, from the bottom of my heart.

Thank you, **Ashley Black**, for sharing your story of courage and determination, for being such an inspiration, and for designing the FasciaBlaster. Your story is one that will continue to inspire others to fight for their dreams and never give up. The FasciaBlaster is an amazing tool that has helped me immensely.

Thank you, **Cierra Lueck,** for sharing your story and enthusiasm. You are so passionate about your work, and I appreciate your willingness to share your knowledge with me and others. Your support has been invaluable, and I am grateful for your friendship.

Inspirations:

I'm so grateful for other artists worldwide as I appreciate all types of art, from painting to music to dance. Their creativity and positive messages remind me there's good in the world and that we can make a difference with our talents and gifts.

Music can be a powerful source of inspiration; positive music is incredibly impactful for me. **FOR KING + COUNTRY** is one of my favorite bands because their music is always so encouraging. I love every song! "Relate," "Broken Halos," "Unity," "H.O.P.E.," "Together," "Burn the Ships," and "God Only Knows" are just a few songs that inspire me. Thank you, Joel and Luke Smallbone, for making such incredible music!

Thank you, **Rebecca St. James,** for your beautiful song "Kingdom Come," which features your brothers, **Joel and Luke Smallbone,** of **For KING & COUNTRY.** It is so powerful and inspiring! Thank you for sharing your talents with the world and using your platform to spread hope and encouragement. Thank you, also, for the positive messages you share.

On those days when everything feels like it's crashing down, and it's hard to see the light at the end of the tunnel, I find comfort in music. One song in particular, "You Say" by **Lauren Daigle,** is relatable and full of hope and encouragement. It reminds me that I am not alone and that I am loved. Thank you, **Lauren Daigle**, for writing such a powerful and beautiful song.

Casting Crowns is another of my favorite bands. Many years ago, I had the pleasure of taking **Mark Hall** and his wife Melanie shopping for their daughter's birthday. From the moment we started talking, I knew we had a special connection. We shared things in common, including working with youth at that time. I quickly learned that they were passionate about their work and loved what they did. I appreciate how **Casting Crowns** uses their music to inspire others, and I am grateful to have had the chance to get to know them better.

The first time I met **Michael W. Smith**, I was struck by his down-to-earth nature. He has such a kind and calm approach to life, and I will never forget how he played with our grandson backstage during a concert break. His music has always been a source of inspiration for me, and I am deeply grateful for his contributions to the world of music. Thank you for sharing your gift with the world.

My Publisher and Team:

Thank you, thank you, thank you! I want to acknowledge **Raymond Aaron, Naval Kumar, Waqas Ahmed, Christina Fife, Lisa Browning, Liz Ventrella**, and everyone involved in the 10-10-10 program. Your contributions have been invaluable in helping me write this book. Without your help, this book would not have been possible. Thank you for your time, effort, and creativity. I am truly grateful. Each of you has helped me to see the world in a new and better way, and I cannot thank you enough.

Finally, I would like to thank everyone who has supported me along the way. Your encouragement has meant so much to me, and I am grateful for your friendship. Thank you all for being a part of my life.

Foreword

Are you living the lifestyle you always envisioned? What if you could tap into a greater power to achieve even more? Have you ever thought about the power of art and nature?

It's no secret that you are the author of your own life. The decisions you make and the actions you take determine your success and happiness.

You might be facing difficulties in your life. Maybe you're dealing with a health issue, or you're going through a tough time financially. Whatever the situation, it is important to remember that you are not alone. Tammy proves that you can overcome anything if you set your mind to it. Despite being diagnosed with brain tumors, and facing other challenges, Tammy never gave up.

I am so excited to endorse Tammy's book, *The Power of Art and Nature*, as it explores how you can use art and nature as a source of healing and inspiration. Drawing on her own experiences, Tammy also shows you how to access your inner power and achieve tremendous success in all areas of your life.

For bonuses go to ...

If you are looking for a way to add more meaning and purpose to your life, this book is must-read. With her insights, practical tips, encouragement and wisdom, Tammy will show you how to tap into the transformative power of art and nature to create the life you've always wanted.

Raymond Aaron
New York Times **Bestselling Author**

Hope for Tomorrow

Chapter 1
Live

1

My Focus

I have always loved nature, being creative, and inspiring others. Spending time outdoors is a must for me. To be honest, I was more of a tomboy growing up. I was raised in a household where everyone pitched in with all the chores. We were taught to ride horses, grow a garden, and how to fish at an early age. My childhood within the home was not by any definition a bed of roses, but I did learn many lessons. Both sets of my grandparents had ranches down in the Klamath Basin of Oregon, and for the first 8 years of my life, I was able to enjoy spending time with them. Their kindness and love have always been an inspiration to me.

When I was around 8 years old, my parents decided to move. We traveled around the Pacific Northwest, including Canada, for six months and finally ended up in Eastern Oregon. In the small town of Enterprise, my dad built our new home. At that time, Enterprise was the booming town in the county.

Now, if you have grown up in a small town, you know it is basically still living in the country. It is true that everyone knows everyone, which is quite nice...most of the time. There are no secrets in a small town. Wallowa County is beautiful, with the backdrop of the Wallowa Mountains. There are many reasons why Chief Joseph loved this place. If you have never been there, I suggest you Google it.

I started earning money by babysitting when I was 12 years old and, in the summers, I worked in the fields. My first investments with the money I earned were a bike and charcoal pencils. I used the brown paper bags from the grocery store to create sketches. What most people do not understand is that we used to recycle and reuse everything back then. Age 14 was the first time I was paid for my art. (I painted windows in storefronts at Christmas time.) Then when I was 16, I worked in a group home for mental patients, which was interesting and rewarding.

It was during my senior year of high school that I met my husband through a mutual friend. A year later, we were married. We wanted to expand our horizons and explore new opportunities. Thankfully, we were given that chance and, as newlyweds, my husband and I moved to the Willamette Valley in Oregon to further our education and to take on new jobs. We started working in property management while attending school. It was there that we started our little family.

I was fortunate to have a flexible schedule, so I had the ability to be a full-time mom, and it gave me the freedom to be creative. Just in case you were wondering, my schooling was in fashion merchandising, design, and color. I love fashion design and I love working with colors. However, sitting behind a sewing machine and sewing all day was not my forte. I did design wedding dresses and different clothing for

4

several years on the side for some little boutiques, but to be honest, I was unfulfilled with sewing.

One day while pushing the stroller in the mall, I got asked if I had ever considered modeling. It turned out to be an agent from Elite modeling (John Casa Blanca), and of course I accepted. This was another opportunity I had always dreamed of! I must admit my focus at 23 was in the fashion industry, modeling, and raising our two lovely daughters. I had a wonderful husband, a fantastic job, and I was doing everything I wanted too! Life finally seemed like it was going perfectly. But it all changed in an instant.

The Fall

I decided in October of 1987 that I would take a job waitressing a few times a week for some extra Christmas money. (Just a note: I am not one for being idle, so I have always done extra things. I have had more part-time jobs and taken more volunteer opportunities than most people have in a lifetime.) I was hired at a busy Chinese restaurant not far from where we lived. The tips were always great, and I liked the work. I should have known that this job was jinxed.

The first night on the job, I tripped going down the stairs carrying a huge tray of food. I was told that they had forgotten to put a new bulb in the stair light. I did not spill anything, but my knee was a different story. I have a high tolerance for pain, but this was more than a little twist that I could shake off. I had our friend, who was a paramedic, check me out. He wrapped it up and told me to schedule an appointment with my doctor. It was swollen and my kneecap moved back and forth. It grossed me out, but I thought, "It is just a sprain; I am fine."

The fall that changed my life was about 2 weeks later. One Friday evening while I was waitressing, a customer came in requesting to speak with the owner. The owner's office was downstairs. I rushed down the stairs and, as I was walking to the office, suddenly my feet slid out from under me. I took a hard fall, hitting my head and back on the concrete floor. Someone had just mopped with greasy, soapy water and forgot to put up any signage to warn anyone about the slippery floor.

I woke up with a throbbing headache and my back was really hurting. I was dazed and in shock. I rested for a few minutes, but I was not feeling any better. I asked to be dismissed for the evening as there was no way I could function anymore that night. I just kept thinking to myself, "I will just go home and rest and tomorrow will be different." I really did not think the fall was as bad as it was. I had had many falls in my life and crashes on my bike growing up that were much worse, or so I thought. I was wrong.

After 67 Doctors' Appointments

The next morning when I awoke, I still had a pounding headache. The worst part was that my memory was gone. I could not remember simple things like names of friends or how to do simple tasks. This development was very frightening.

I made an appointment to see a doctor. Since this was an on-the-job injury, I had to see a Workman's Comp doctor. The first 3 doctors that I saw did not listen to me or take me seriously. They acted like I was delusional, and they would not even look at my knee. They did not believe I could have a constant headache for days or that I had any memory loss. After those experiences, I did not care who I saw. I just needed a doctor who would actually listen to me.

To be honest, I do not remember everything exactly, but I remember I was scared and confused. My only advice from the doctors was, "You probably have a slight concussion. Take some Tylenol and rest."

During this time, I went to see a chiropractor for my back. He referred me to an orthopedic surgeon. It was frustrating and confusing when my insurance and Workman's Comp were fighting over who would cover me medically. Thankfully, I found an experienced legal team who represented me and got me the help I needed. I would never have thought I would need a lawyer to get medical attention.

Finally, I was starting to get treatment and physical therapy 3–5 times a week. The first day of treatment, my physical therapist looked at me with a confused expression. "How long did it take them to get you out of the car?" she asked. "Certainly, they must have had to use the jaws of life." I just smiled and replied, "Nope, just a fall." I could see the wheels turning in her head as she tried to make sense of my response. A fall might seem like no big deal, but it can have profound consequences. My neurologist told me, "If you hit your head in the wrong spot when falling, it could easily kill you. After 6 months, I still had bruising on the back of my brain.

After 67 doctors' appointments, x-rays, MRIs, physical therapy, and all kinds of different tests, I was diagnosed with brain tumors, fibromyalgia, and severe nerve damage. I was told that I would not live very much longer or that I would be totally crippled before I turned 35. I was told I would never be able to create my art or do gardening ever again. Surgery was not an option for me because of where the tumors were located, and there was less than a 5% chance I would survive the surgery. Although I was terrified, I was thankful to finally have an answer. It still had not hit me how bad it really was. And I had the daunting task of figuring out how to tell my husband and young daughters that our lives were forever changed.

Looking at Their Little Faces

What? What did he say? I have brain tumors. My first question to the doctor was, "Well, are they cancerous?" They did not know. I was told it would take 2 to 3 weeks for that answer. I remember telling my husband and watching his reaction. What made me cry was seeing in his eyes the fear and sadness. I was not afraid of dying, but I was sad for him. He could potentially lose his wife, the mother of his children. I tried to keep the conversation positive and told him we would know more after the pending test results were in. Then, we would deal with it. No matter the challenge, I would always tell myself that "with God, all things are possible." This simple phrase has always given me the strength and courage to face any situation.

It is hard to describe how I felt looking at my daughters' faces each morning. It was a mixture of so many emotions. I wondered if I would ever get to see them grow up and experience all the wonderful things life has to offer (go to school, graduate, get married, or have children of their own). I had no idea what was in store for me or all of us. All I wanted was more time with my husband and my girls. I just had to trust that everything would work out in the end.

I honestly did not want anyone to know what was happening with me. I did not want anyone to feel sorry for me. Besides, the few I did tell did not believe me. Doctors did not even believe me unless they saw the MRIs or read my file. How could I really expect anyone else to believe me, much less understand what I was going through?

The greatest thing my experience through all of this has taught me is understanding how many people are going through devastating illnesses and diagnoses, like cancer, MS, lupus, diabetes, and other debilitating, invisible diseases and illnesses, and how brave they are. Just remember that just because someone does not look sick, it does not mean they are not ill. It does not mean they are faking their diagnosis. Be kind. I have found that most people dealing with severe illnesses try to hide it bravely. Instead, they choose to fight silently or with a few trusted people in their lives. Have you ever noticed that people with minor illnesses often are the loudest whiners? This is because they have not dealt with the hard things that ultimately are life changing. So, remember to be kind the next time you see or interact with someone with a debilitating or invisible illness. You never know what somebody else is going through.

Another interesting fact I have learned through this process is that many doctors do not believe women when they say they are ill. Why is that? Is it because most women are so good at prioritizing other people before themselves? Have you ever dealt with a severe illness or had a family member or friend diagnosed with cancer, tumors, MS, or some other serious disease? How did it make you feel? What was your reaction?

You May Not Wake Up

It was weeks before we got the test results back on my tumors. The waiting for my final diagnosis of cancer or no cancer seemed to take forever. What would I do if it was cancer? Is there a need for me to be concerned? I didn't think so…but again, I was wrong.

During this time of waiting, I experienced every emotion. I knew in my heart, though, I needed to change my attitude so that I could be prepared for the worst-case scenario. I knew that a negative attitude would not help me or anyone around me. I needed to be positive and optimistic to face any challenges that may lie ahead.

We finally got the news that the tumors were not cancerous. Yes! It was great news! My fears started to alleviate. I was thinking, "Yes! There is a chance I could recover from this. My headaches and dizziness will disappear, and I will get stronger."

During this time, my husband and I started thinking about life insurance. We contacted our insurance agent, signed all the forms, and thought everything was taken care of. A few weeks later, I received a call from our agent. This call was when the reality hit me of how sick I was. He said that they could not insure me. In shock, I asked him, "What do you mean?" He told me that after having an expert review my medical charts, they could not insure me. Again, I asked, "Why not? Are you sure? Not for any policy?" He said, "No, I am sorry. The medical expert said you might not wake up tomorrow." I did not know what to say or how to process what he had just said to me. I thanked him and hung up the phone.

My first thought was, "No one knows how long they will live; only God knows." Immediately, the Bible verse "With God, all things are possible" popped into my head. I was in shock and tears. I was scared now. In my mind, I could hear people saying, "You must have done something wrong," "You deserve this," and "God is punishing you." Have you ever heard these things being said before? So, I knew it was time to start praying and have an honest and genuine conversation with God.

Live Another Day

"Why me, God? Why won't my headaches go away, God? God, I know you have a purpose for me being here, but what is it? Thank you for all you have given me, but please let me live another day!" As you can see, my prayers went from frustration to anger to thankfulness. I had a talented team of doctors. I was told they were using me in a worldwide study so that they would find something. At least, even if it could not help me, maybe it would help someone else. They experimented with many different treatments, but nothing worked. I felt like an experiment gone wrong.

The doctors tried, and they cared, but nothing seemed to work. I would take one medicine, then need to take another to counteract the reaction. Finally, I would have a bad reaction and end up in the hospital. On a pain scale of 1 to 10, my pain was always a 7 to 10—painful and not fun, and that was just the headaches. If you have ever had a bad migraine, that hints at what they were like.

I was sicker than anyone knew, and honestly, at times, I felt like I was dying. I felt like my head would explode from the pressure. Tests and more tests, and more therapy; they even sent me to a pain clinic. Nothing seemed to work.

I recall my sister-in-law going with me to one pain clinic appointment. I was told I needed to avoid certain foods because they could trigger headaches. You should have seen the list. All we could do was laugh, as it would have been better if they had given me a list of what I could eat and drink. As I recall, water and lettuce was okay.

I did learn that keeping busy kept my mind off my pain. I also realized that no matter how sick I was, I needed to move daily. So, I kept busy, not only working full time, taking care of our girls, and teaching art, but I also spent time tending my garden and volunteering, to help keep my mind off the pain. I was so tired of the testing, being sick, and feeling crippled, but I realized a bad attitude would not get me anywhere. So, I told myself, "I am going to live each day as if it is my last." Now, exactly what else did I need to change?

Longbridge at Sunset

Chapter 2
Change

2

Vacations Weren't Enough

first thought we needed to take mini vacations at least once a month, if not every weekend. Most of our weekends were filled with our daughters' activities during the school year. In the summertime, we spent our weekends getting outdoors and spending time in nature—camping, backpacking, or boating. We had three weeks a year of paid vacation, and we enjoyed each one to the fullest. We loved traveling all around the Northwest. We were able to spend time with family and friends and explore unfamiliar places. It was a time to relax and enjoy life and each other.

I did not enjoy that it seemed like I had to work double the hours to prepare to leave, and triple when we got back. I swear there were at least ten new problems that needed resolving. Have you ever felt that way? Of course, by resolving those ten problems and everything else, you are wondering why you came back. Of course, we loved our vacations. But we realized vacations just were not enough.

We realized we needed to do something different, something more. We were missing something. What was it?

Stress

Stress is the silent killer. That may seem like an extreme statement, but is it? Think about it... Stress affects us emotionally, psychologically, and physically. How does it affect us emotionally or psychologically? Anger, frustration, forgetfulness, difficulty making decisions, lack of motivation, depression, mood swings, anxiety, and many other symptoms. How does it affect you physically? Have you ever thought about this? It can cause difficulty breathing, dry skin, increased heart rate, heart attacks, and strokes. Even headaches and hair loss are attributed to stress because stress attacks the immune system.

Have you ever been stressed out? I know I have. It is just not fun. Are you in a stressful situation? I think sometimes we do not realize how much stress we are under. Have you ever noticed that stress comes from being around negative people, being in a hostile environment, or simply watching or reading something negative? Stress often shows us how important it is to choose our friends wisely and where to spend our time, including what type of lifestyle we want. It reminds me of a children's song with these lyrics: "Be careful little ears what you hear; be careful little eyes what you see." It is true... we need to watch what we see and hear and who we spend our valuable time with.

The truth is, I was getting sicker, not better. So, I met with one of my doctors. His words were: "Stress is killing you; you need change. You need to live in a stress-free environment." Honestly, I knew he was right, but how would I accomplish this? It seems like most of us are surrounded by one stressful situation after another. Have you ever noticed this in your life? Finally, I understood we needed something to change.

Change Is Good

Change is something that we all go through in life. It is a necessary part of growth and development. Yet, for some reason, most people are afraid of change. Fear is the primary reason we resist change, even though it is sometimes reasonable and necessary. Change comes in many forms—a change in our diet, exercise routine, job, house, or a new location. Sometimes you need a complete life makeover.

This was me. I finally realized that I needed a complete life makeover. I needed something new and different. But what was it that I needed to do to initiate this change? I started evaluating my life. Did I need to change my diet? No. I already ate highly healthy. Did I need more exercise? No. I exercised several hours 5 days a week. Was I happy with my job? Not especially. Was I happy with my home or where we lived? To be honest, I hated living in an apartment. I wanted our own home. I wanted to have a home in a peaceful environment where I felt like our girls would be safe and have room to run and explore.

After much discussion, we thought the best thing would be to look for a vacation home. Someplace we could go to get away from everything. Someplace we could eventually call home. First, we made a list of what we wanted to look for. Where do we want to live? What kind of atmosphere or lifestyle do we want? Do we want to live near the ocean, forest, lake, or river?

We decided we wanted to live someplace we would choose as a vacation destination. Someplace with easy access to fly out to warmer climates if necessary. We wanted to be somewhere with four seasons. For the next year, we spent every available weekend looking for that perfect place. We traveled around Oregon, California, Washington, Idaho, Montana, and even Western Canada. It wasn't until we started crossing the Long Bridge into Sandpoint, Idaho, that we felt this was where we were meant to be.

One important thing to remember about change is that no age limit or circumstance cannot be overcome by courage. At various stages of our lives, there will always be the need to see the necessity of change and be brave enough to chase it with all our might.

We needed to be sure that this choice was God's best place for us. Also, we needed the courage to make a move.

Country Road

The Move

We spent a week in Northern Idaho looking for the perfect vacation home or property. We boated around all the beautiful lakes in the area and drove miles around Bonner and Kootenai counties. I took numerous vacation photos of our girls playing in and around the water and having so much fun. I only took one photo of property out of the many places we saw. We fell in love with the property and the potential we saw there. It turned out to be the place we would eventually build our lovely home. We made an offer and, after assuring the owner that we were a family and not a developer (she required a picture of our family), she accepted our offer. I knew immediately I wanted to move here, but to be honest, it did not look like that would happen any time soon.

The doubt and questions started pouring in. Who would give up a good paying job/career, with housing and insurance, and move somewhere with no job security and no home, with two little girls? This was not an area close to family or friends or where we even grew up. This was hundreds of miles away from everything and everyone we had ever known. I remember people asking, "Why would God want you to live there?" But I knew in my heart, this was where God wanted us to be. Still, as all of us often do, we started doubting our decision.

Have you ever been in a place where there are significant decisions to be made that you already know the answers to, but because of the loud voices of others, you start doubting yourself? Usually, this doubt comes from family and friends questioning your choices. But, again, doubt comes from fear of the unknown. Many times, uncertainty comes from what we have been taught about ourselves.

It takes bravery to overcome these fears. We must believe in ourselves and throw aside the need to please others or accept what they say about us. We need to step out of closed boxes and welcome the new. Remember when I was telling you that sometimes we need change? Well, my friends, sometimes we need to take a chance.

We did just that and moved. We took the chance. It was not easy, yet the challenges were fun and rewarding. We have no regrets, except we wish we had made a move earlier. Are you where you want to be, or do you need to be brave and take a chance?

New Surroundings

As I looked around at our new surroundings, I felt incredibly blessed. We were surrounded by a beautiful forest with various trees—cedar, fir, pine, tamarack, aspen, and birch. There was a small meadow with wildflowers like daisies, Indian paintbrush, and other lovely blooms. And everywhere I looked, wild ferns and huckleberries were growing under the trees. It was the place I had always dreamed of finding, and it could not have come at a better time. Instead of the daily noise of cars and people, all I could hear was the chirping of squirrels, the songs of birds, and the occasional woodpecker knocking on a tree. It was perfect.

One thing was missing—flowing water. We had a seasonal creek, but I loved the sound of running water. It is calming to the soul. So, I took it upon myself to install a small pond and stream. Besides, if Grandma could do it, so could I. Through the years, we have added several ponds and waterfalls throughout our landscape. The addition of water has not only enhanced the beauty of our property; it has also provided a haven for wildlife. Frogs, fish, and dragonflies are just a few creatures that have made our ponds their home. And watching them brings me joy. Whenever I see a bird bathing in the stream or a butterfly flitting over the waterfall, I am reminded of the simple pleasure flowing water can bring.

We had always hoped to see a moose in our backyard but never thought it would happen. One day, during the building process, our small daughters were spending time together at our "campsite." Suddenly, we heard screaming from both our girls. As I hurried down the ladder, I could see them running and screaming down the driveway...followed by a baby moose trotting behind them like a big puppy. The girls had been sitting around the campfire when our oldest daughter felt something on her shoulder. When she looked up, she realized it was this baby moose. Startled and scared, she jumped up, threw down the pillow she was holding, and ran with her sister. We found dirty moose prints on the pillow she had thrown down. So, we now have a hysterical story about our first wild moose experience. Although it was a scary situation, we now look back and laugh at how fast our girls ran away from the friendly moose. These moments make us realize how blessed we are to live in such a beautiful place where wild creatures roam freely.

As I look around our home, I am grateful for my husband's vision and willingness to take on the massive task of building our home. He has a keen eye for detail and can translate my ideas into reality. He is truly a skilled artisan, and his workmanship is impeccable. People often underestimate the work and artistry that goes into building a house. It is truly a labor of love. Our home reflects our shared vision, and I am proud of what we have created together. I hope that we can inspire others to follow their dreams and create their own beautiful homes.

Just as we need to take care of our physical bodies with the proper food and exercise, our minds also need diligent care. Too often, we allow outside influences to dictate how we think and feel. We are exposed to so much negativity daily that it can be easy to forget what makes us happy. We must take time for ourselves and ask ourselves the tough questions. What kind of people do we want to surround ourselves with? What kind of lifestyle do we want to live? Answering these questions can be difficult, but creating the life we want is necessary. Our homes are an extension of ourselves, so they must reflect our inner peace and joy. If they do not, it may be time for a change. Consider making changes in your life that will lead you to a more peaceful tomorrow.

Do You Need Change?

Do you need change? It is a simple question but does not always have a simple answer. You need to reevaluate where you are, both physically and mentally. Ask yourself some honest questions. Do you need to change something significant or something small? Maybe you just need to change your attitude or a bad habit.

Here are some questions you may want to ask. What is it that I need to change? Am I working in an area that I enjoy? Do I like living here? Am I happy? Am I living the lifestyle I have always wanted? What am I doing to achieve that? How is my attitude toward my work, relationships, colleagues, and family? Do I have any unhealthy habits/addictions that are impeding my progress? This could be as simple as being on your cell phone and neglecting personal interactions.

Something I always do before I make a change is to consider how my choices /decisions will affect those around me. Everything we do or say ultimately affects others. People often do not think about this, especially when we are focused on our work or achievements. Everyone lives in different circumstances. There is a song, "Relate," from the Christian Group "For King and Country" that says ... "I don't know what it's like to be you, you don't know what it's like to be me...What if we're all the same in different kinds of ways? Can you, can you relate?" I try to consider these thoughts when I deal with others.

Making changes in your life can be a daunting task. You want to be sure that your choices are positive ones that will have a lasting impact on your life and the lives of those around you. However, with careful planning and thought, you can make changes that will bring joy and peace into your life while improving your health and lifestyle. By thinking about what you want out of life, you can make choices that will lead you down the path to happiness and fulfillment. So, when considering making any change in your life, be sure to take the time to do it right. The rewards will be well worth the effort.

You are the product of your environment. The people you surround yourself with have a profound impact on your life. If you are surrounded by negative people who put you down, you will start to doubt yourself. You will begin to believe you are not good enough and will never achieve your dreams. But if you surround yourself with positive, ambitious people, you will start to believe in yourself. You will begin to see the possibilities for your life. You'll be inspired to achieve remarkable things. So, if you want to change your life, start by changing the people you spend time with. Spend more time with the people who inspire you and make you feel good about yourself, and spend less time with the people who bring you down.

Chosen

Chapter 3
Inspiration

3

Go Where You are Inspired

When you get up in the morning, what inspires you? Do you look outside? Go for a walk or work out? Listen to music? I am curious to know what inspires you each day. Do you get up, grab a coffee, and turn the TV on? Is it positive energy? Are you motivated for the day or want to crawl back into bed? Think about it; where does your inspiration come from each day? Are you inspired by sitting still with a delightful book, enjoying a cup of coffee or tea? We all need some type of inspiration.

I start my day thanking God for a new day before climbing out of bed. Some of you will understand this, but others may ask why. It is like this... I woke up today! I survived another night, and now I am blessed to live another day. Do you get that? Each day we wake up is a gift. Let me repeat this... *Each day we wake up is a gift!* Each day is worthy of celebration! Not everything is perfect, but you will find something good each day if you look for it. Since you have been given this gift of another day, you should do something positive to help someone, even if that "someone" is yourself!

Once I am out of bed for the day, it is time for a cup of coffee or chai tea and to search for my daily inspiration. But, of course, I do not follow the same routine every day; close, but not the same. Inspiration usually comes when we are actively pursuing it. The pursuit of inspiration will usually lead us to a place where our hearts find calmness and peace, which will motivate us to continue seeking ways to better ourselves.

What is it that you need to do? Use your senses. Listen to the sounds around you. Can you hear the waves crashing against the shore or the sound of a squirrel chirping in a nearby tree? Close your eyes and smell the scents around you. Can you smell the rain in the air or the flowers along the sidewalk? Simply touch a wildflower or put your toes in the water or sand. Can you feel the sand's grittiness or the water's coolness on your skin? Can you feel the silky softness or prickles on your fingertips? What do you see as you look around your surroundings? Look hard; you may be missing something magical and inspiring. Simply put, you need to go where you are inspired.

One of my favorite ways to recreate inspiration is through my art. I use a variety of mediums and techniques to create each unique and custom piece. Each piece is a realistic re-creation of the nature I see. I love to bring the outdoors inside, as it creates a sense of relaxation. This is one way I can inspire others.

One of the stories of how my art inspires others is from my client/friend Pam. One day I was picking up a gorgeous bouquet of roses for our granddaughter's dance recital; I just had to create a 3-D sculpture of the roses. It is called "Chosen." My husband asked why I had decided to make this piece. I just told him God laid it on my heart, as it was meant for someone we do not even know yet. I was right. When I met Pam, it was at the hospital, where she greeted my husband for his surgery. I showed Pam a few photos of what I do, and one was of this rose sculpture. After that, whenever we met, or I posted a picture on my social media, she loved it and commented, "That is my piece." A year later, she purchased it. This 3-D oil wall sculpture now hangs in her beautiful home. It brings back memories of her childhood in her grandmother's rose garden and gives her joy and comfort each time she looks at it... Everyone should have art that motivates or brings back a good memory, art that inspires.

I know that having art reflects nature, and spending time in nature gives me renewed energy and inspiration.

Nature Is Inspiring

Nature is inspiring and powerful. For me, it is not just a desire but an actual necessity! Have you ever thought about the healing powers of nature? If you think about it, nature provides us with clean air, soil, water, plants, trees, food, and everything we need to survive. So, people should go to nature for healing. There are multiple studies on the healing powers of nature and how it reduces the symptoms of anxiety, stress, cancer, heart issues, depression, and many other diseases.*

Think about it; where do you go for vacation? Is it a tropical island? Playtime at the beach? Some type of resort? Floating down a river?

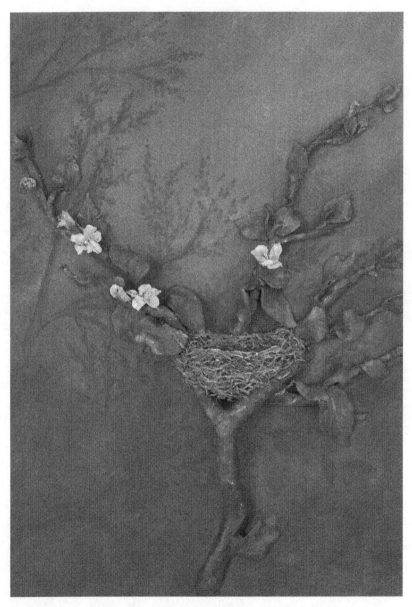

New Beginnings

Camping in the mountains? Do you spend your vacation time in nature or a shopping mall?

I am not saying that city life can't be fun, but when you are stuck in an office all day looking at a computer screen, is that fun? Do you go outside, and everything is concrete, traffic, and noise? Do you ever just want to get away? Where do you go and what do you do for relaxation? Truthfully, if I had to sit in front of a computer screen all day long, it would feel like I was in prison. I need to have peace and quiet.

My inspiration and my peace come from the enchanting wonders of nature—the trickling of a stream, the whispering of the leaves in the wind, a majestic rise of a mountain range, or the simple sound of a hummingbird's wings hovering over a sweet lily. My mission: To enhance people's lives through the creation of beautiful art that causes them to reflect, imagine, and be inspired.

This reminds me of a story. A few years ago, I was inspired by the little songbirds at our place to create a 3D wall sculpture. "New Beginnings" is a sculpted 3D oil painting of a nest in an apple tree. When I was painting it, a gorgeous little yellow finch landed on my easel, where it sang me a song. I was amazed and blessed to have this encounter with the sweetness of nature.

Even though I live in the forest, I sometimes need to get away for the day. One of my favorite places on a warm summer day is out on the lake. It is hard to explain, but somehow, I forget about everything else. Instead, I am focused on what I can see, smell, and feel. As the gentle waves crash on the shoreline, we watch the golden eagles flying overhead; the fresh air always smells so good with the hint of pine. I dip my toes in the cool water, which is so inviting, while the sun shines down and touches my skin; the stress and anxiety of daily life is melted away.

Outside, everything is so fresh and new. The sun is shining, and the birds are singing. You can smell the flowers and the trees. The wind is blowing through your hair. You feel so alive! Nature has a way of making you feel good, doesn't it? It is like it has its own healing powers. And that is why I love spending time in my gardens.

*The Healing Power of Nature | Psychology Today
https://www.psychologytoday.com › the-roots-health
*The Healing Power of Nature – Hidden River
https://hiddenriverhealing.com › the-healing-power-of-...

In the Garden

I have planted seeds and flowers for as long as I can remember. My first memories of planting in the garden were at my grandparents' place. I recall the large rows of vegetable plants: kohlrabi, peas, carrots, beans, corn, beets, tomatoes, and other veggies. My grandparents also had fields filled with potatoes. Besides having a huge vegetable garden and an orchard, my grandmother had a large yard with beautiful flower gardens. It was breathtaking, and it provided immense joy to all of us. Planting seeds is such a magical thing. You take these tiny little seeds, add some water and soil, and

Under the Vines

then watch in amazement as they sprout and grow into beautiful plants. It is an excellent way to connect with nature and the cycle of life.

You may be wondering if I have a garden. Of course, several! My vegetable gardens have special fencing to keep out deer, elk, rabbits, and moose. (These amazing animals can do a lot of damage.) We have raspberries, grapes, strawberries, and chives and other herbs that come back yearly. We also have a small orchard in the garden: apples, plums, cherries, and pears. Every spring, I plant seeds and vegetables in the planter boxes my husband built for me. I love going outside and discovering what is happening in the garden. Every day, there is something new to see. The other day, I found a frog sunning itself on a leaf. Today, I saw a butterfly flitting from flower to flower. Spending time in the garden surrounded by nature is always a joy.

In the springtime, my flower gardens come to life. The bees start buzzing, and the butterflies flutter about. The dragonflies dart through the air, and the hummingbirds come to visit. I love spending time in the gardens, discovering all the different flowers that are in bloom. Each day, there is something new to see. The colors are so vibrant, and the fragrance is intoxicating. I cannot help but feel happy when I am surrounded by such beauty. It's no wonder that flowers have been known to lift people's spirits. I am so lucky to have a place where I can go to escape the hustle and bustle of everyday life and simply enjoy the natural world.

Many people see gardening as a chore that needs to be done to have a nice-looking yard. But there is so much more to it than that. Gardening is a way to connect with nature, get your hands dirty, and discover the hidden beauty in the world around us. In the garden, we can find peace and solace or come together with friends and family to laugh and enjoy each other's company. And, of course, there is nothing quite like the taste of a freshly picked tomato or the smell of a beautiful bouquet of flowers. So next time you feel stressed or down, take some time outside and dig in the dirt. You just might be surprised at how good it makes you feel.

Every day, I discover something new in the gardens. The flowers bloom, the vegetables thrive, and the herbs are ready for harvest. I cannot wait to get started on my next meal!

Garden to Table

Garden to table is about more than just picking vegetables for dinner. It is about discovering the joy of gardening and using that fresh produce to create a beautiful, artful meal. It's about spending time outside in nature, getting your hands dirty, and being inspired by the Earth's bounty.

What could be more fun than picking fresh herbs from your own garden? With just a little time and effort, you can discover the joys of gardening and enjoy the delicious flavors of fresh-picked herbs. Basil, mint, oregano, rosemary, and thyme are just a few delightful herbs that can add flavor to your favorite recipes. And there is nothing like the smell of fresh basil in your kitchen!

Can you imagine how nice it would be to know where your food comes from? If you take the time to grow your own food, you can be confident in its freshness and quality. There is something so special about food that is grown with your own two hands. When you take the time to plant, water, and care for a garden, the sense of satisfaction and accomplishment is unlike any other. Not to mention, it is a great way to exercise and spend time in nature. But beyond the physical benefits, gardening can also be a terrific way to reduce stress and anxiety. Nurturing something else can be incredibly therapeutic, giving you a sense of purpose and helping you feel more connected to the world around you.

There is nothing quite like the smell of a garden: fresh, earthy, and impressive. You are instantly transported to a different world when you step into a garden; a world where the colors are brighter, the smells are more robust, and the tastes are more vibrant. It's a world where you can discover new things about yourself and the world around you.

One of my favorite things to do in the garden is to smell the tomatoes. Tomato plants have the same scent as the tomatoes they produce, yet tomatoes have no smell when purchased from the grocery store. It is fascinating to think about how much flavor and aroma are lost in mass production. Another example is strawberries grown fresh; you could eat them green and they would taste sweeter than those you buy in the store. When you grow your own food or flowers, you will learn to appreciate all the farmers (including yourself) that provide healthy food. Not to mention, it is just enjoyable to walk outside and pick up your dinner (or lunch or breakfast) right off the plant!

I think one of the best parts about summer is discovering all the different fruits and vegetables that are in season. Whether you grow them yourself or buy them from a farmer's market, there is something special about enjoying produce at the peak of ripeness. And what could be better than preserving some of that bounty to enjoy later in the year? I love making small-batch specialty items like strawberry jam, raspberry jelly, and applesauce. I also like to get creative with savory sauces like pizza and enchilada. And my all-time favorite is zucchini relish. It is versatile and adds a delicious flavor to anything from sandwiches to salads. If you have never preserved your food before, I recommend trying it. It is a fun way to experiment with new flavors and enjoy the taste of summer all year long!

Living in Northern Idaho, we are privileged to be surrounded by the natural beauty of the forest. We discover the hidden wonders that most people never get to see daily. Whether taking a stroll through our landscape and gardens or spotting wildlife on a hike, we are constantly reminded of how lucky we are to live in such a beautiful place. The forest is a never-ending source of inspiration, and we are grateful to be able to call it our home.

Flowers and Wildlife

The function of a home is to provide shelter, but the beauty of a home is that it can be so much more. A home can be a sanctuary, a place to escape the hustle and bustle of everyday life. It can be a canvas, a blank slate waiting to be filled with your distinctive touch. From the moment you drive up, you know this is a special place. Our home and landscape flow together and combine with the natural vegetation around us. There are ponds and streams with waterfalls, all of which create a peaceful environment, and it was all intentional.

We only took out trees that were necessary for building our home, because we wanted to preserve as much of the existing forest as possible. The woods are essential to our landscape, inspiring my

Wild Daisy

artwork immensely. Some of our trees are over 100 years old, including a cedar grove. I love walking through the landscape and finding inspiration for my art. The trees, plants, songbirds, and wildlife have all made their way into my pieces. By creating this space, we have not only enhanced our property; we have also created a place where I can walk out my door and be inspired to create art.

The wildlife is attracted to this natural landscape, and I believe they know it is our little wildlife preserve. At any given time, you will find frogs in the pond, a bird taking a bath in the stream, or deer hidden in the grass. The turkeys like to bring their young into the yard early in the mornings. I love watching them while I drink my coffee. It is funny how they walk back and forth searching for bugs. The wildlife is not afraid of us, especially moose when they occasionally visit. They seem to sense that we mean no harm and are there to protect them. In many ways, these natural wonders are like a little piece of heaven on earth, and I am lucky to have them right in my backyard.

We have wildflowers that blossom early in the springtime alongside the flowers I have planted, like tulips, daffodils, iris, peonies, astilbe, and others. The natural ferns usually appear at the end of May, and the wild honeysuckle bloom in June. The wildflowers on our acreage and in our area are spectacular. It seems like there is always something blooming. You will see lupine, wild roses, honeysuckles, daisies, and other pretty flowers. I realize these flowers are considered weeds to some people, but to me, they are so pretty. They are simply wildflowers.

Forests are one of my favorite places to explore. There is something about being surrounded by all the trees and flowers that makes me feel at peace. And you never know what you will discover on a hike through the forest. I have encountered hidden lakes, cascading waterfalls, and secluded meadows, all teeming with wildlife. The smell of the woods is also one of my favorite things. It is like a mixture of pine and soil that makes me feel alive.

I am not sure if you have ever noticed the trees that grow on cliffs or rocks, but it is impressive. It is hard for most plants to thrive with good soil and water—what about those goats who climb up high? They must be brave! From time to time, as I think about them, my determination increases even more so, because this life journey seems daunting (but manageable once we consider our own perseverance). These natural environments provide excellent opportunities for incredible photos. Yet, there are other places I like to travel to for inspiration. There are so many unique and beautiful places around you, your state, and the world that will give you inspiration and can be captured in a photo.

Taking the Shot

I am truly blessed to live in an area surrounded by natural beauty. From the pristine lakes and forests to the rushing rivers, there is always something to explore and admire. And each time I visit these places, they look slightly different due to the changing seasons and light. That is why I make it a point to take plenty of photos whenever I go somewhere new. Some people may laugh at how many pictures I take, but I know that each one captures a unique moment that may never be repeated. After all, nature is constantly changing, and you never know what tomorrow may bring. A natural or man-made disaster could completely alter the landscape, so it is important to take the shot while you can. So go ahead and snap away! Inspire others with your artistry and enjoy the simple beauty of nature.

Reflections (Glacier National Park)

There is something magical about discovering unfamiliar places. It is like opening a new door to an unknown world, and you never know what you will find on the other side. For me, exploration is all about the journey. I love getting lost in unfamiliar places and seeing where the wind takes me. There are so many hidden gems out there waiting to be discovered, and it is important to take the time to explore them. Not only are there photo opportunities galore, but you never know when you might stumble upon something truly special.

I am sure each person has their own personal favorite type to visit, but no matter what kind it may entail—whether its hiking through forests surrounded by lush greenery, or relaxing under a tree—we just need to take the time to discover them.

There is something about being in nature that just instantly makes me feel more creative and inspired. Maybe it's the fresh air, or the wide-open spaces, but whatever it is, I always find myself feeling more imaginative when I am surrounded by natural beauty. That is why I love to visit places like Glacier National Park, the Oregon Coast, and Hawaii. Each of these destinations offers its own unique brand of inspiration, and I never come home from a trip without a head full of innovative ideas.

I love the Oregon Coast. Can you imagine the excitement of your first glimpse of the ocean? The water and waves seem to go on forever. The salty smell of the ocean air is distinct and welcoming. It brings anticipation of all the wonders that I am about to absorb. I love walking barefoot and feeling the warm sand between my toes. The sound comes next...the crashing waves on the beach or against the rocks. I have often noticed that when it is storming, the waves crashing against the rocks or cliffs of a lighthouse roar like thunder. The power of the ocean is magnificent. It is frightening and beautiful at the same time. Yet, I always feel God's presence there. Whether it is stormy or calm, I never have to search too hard for unique photos. Inspiration seems to be everywhere I look. Anticipation builds as I wait for just the right moment to take the shot. The sight and sound of sand and waves combine to create a feeling of peace and serenity that is unmatched anywhere else on Earth.

As an artist, I am always in search of inspiration. And there is no shortage of inspiration to be found in Glacier National Park. From the moment you arrive, you are surrounded by natural beauty. Whether you spend your days rafting the river or hiking the trails, there is always something new to discover. And of course, Going-to-the-Sun Road is a photographer's paradise. The last time I visited, the road had just opened for the summer season. The light was perfect, and I was able to take some amazing pictures. If you go to my website, mitzkafinearts.com, you will see what I mean. The pictures are proof that sometimes all you need is talent and a little bit of luck. Who knows, maybe someday one of my pictures will inspire someone else to visit Glacier National Park.

There is something special about Hawaii that cannot be found anywhere else in the world. The talents and gifts of the people who live on these islands is unique and inspiring. From the moment you step foot on the sand, you can feel the warmth of the water and the sun. The sea life is incredible and there is always something new to discover. The tropical foliage is unlike anything else, and the colors are so vibrant. We have been lucky enough to snorkel with dolphins every time we have gone, and it is an amazing experience. They are such talented creatures, and it is a true gift to be able to swim with them. We also love going kayaking and swimming in the waves. The ocean is always fascinating and there are so many interesting things to see, both underwater and above. Hawaii is truly a place like no other.

Each of these places is unique in its own ways, just as we are all unique in our own ways. We just need to take the time to discover this.

Princess Moonlight

Chapter 4
Uniqueness

Discovering Me

D iscovering me? Yes, that is what I needed to do! Who am I? I never had asked myself this question before; it wasn't until I was told that I may not live that I started looking at myself, trying to discover who I was. We think we know who we are, or do we? Do we just listen to what everyone else says and agree with them, assuming they know us? Do you know what happens when you assume? It is not good!

I started looking at all aspects of my life: the family I come from, the friends I have, what I like and don't like. This took a lot of time and soul searching but it was worth it. Inspiration comes from many places, some unique to each person. For me, discovering who I was, meant finding out what made me unique and using that to inspire others. If we all took the time to discover ourselves, the world would be a more inspiring place!

It is not something that happens overnight. It is basically soul searching. Spending time alone in nature, like taking a walk, helps with this step. Something else that helps is serving others. We tend to find our strengths when we help others. So, how did I start to discover myself? First, I started asking myself questions. Here are a few I started with: What are the most essential things in my life? What are my values? What would I want to do if this was my last day on Earth? Who do I like spending time with? What is my journey? These were tough questions for me to answer at first, because I had never really taken the time to think about them before. But once I started thinking about them, it was like a switch went off in my brain and everything became clear to me.

Answering these questions helped me to realize what was tremendously important to me and what I should be striving for in life. It also helped me to identify the people who were positive influences in my life and those who were not. Asking myself these tough questions was a key step in discovering myself. Another crucial step was spending time alone in nature. This allowed me to clear my mind and just focus on the present moment.

Being in nature also helped me to connect with something larger than myself and appreciate the beauty of the world around me.

Lastly, serving others was another key step in discovering myself. Helping others made me feel good and motivated me to continue doing charitable deeds. It also showed me that I can make a difference in the world, which was something I had not fully realized before. So those are just a few of the steps I took on my journey of self-discovery. If you are feeling lost or stuck in life, these steps will help you too!

One of my favorite songs to listen to during challenging times is by artist Lauren Daigle: "You Say." The first line starts with: "I keep fighting voices in my mind that say I'm not enough." Inspiration comes in all shapes and sizes. Maybe, for you, it is a song, a color, or a sunset. Maybe it's the way your best friend always knows just what to say, or your little sister's contagious laugh. In whichever way it comes to you, let it fill you up so you can overflow into the rest of the world.

Inspiration is meant to be shared! The more unique each of us are, the more we have to offer. So do not be afraid to be yourself and let your light shine! Inspiration is all around us...we just must be open to discovering it. Who knows, maybe you'll even inspire someone else today. Take the time to get to know yourself; you may be surprised at what you find!

It's Okay to Be You

It's okay to be you! Now, sometimes that is the hardest thing to accept. It is because we are not confident. So let us look at confidence.

What is confidence? Confidence means feeling sure of yourself and your abilities; not in an arrogant way but in a realistic, secure way. Confidence is not about feeling superior to others. It is a quiet inner knowledge that you are capable. Confident people feel secure rather than insecure (kidshealth.org).

Confidence—such a small word with such a big meaning—is something we all strive for and yet often find ourselves falling short of. Why is that? Lack of confidence usually results from something negative in our past. We were told we were not good enough, pretty enough, too skinny, or too fat; we were told we could not or should not or were simply just made fun of. My question is, who do they think they are? Do people really think it is okay to tear someone down? I heard these comments growing up, and I still hear them today. There is no denying it; it can hit us hard. It tears at our hearts and has us second guessing things we know how to do, or who we really are. It can make us doubt our talent, our gift, our unique ability to contribute something special to this world. But here is the thing: We are all special. We all have something to offer that is unlike anyone else. So, the next time you find yourself lacking confidence, remember that you are talented, you are gifted, and you are uniquely qualified to do remarkable things in this world. Stand tall and be proud of who you are. We need YOU!

So how do we build our self-confidence and get out of this rut?

1. First, look in the mirror and realize God has you here for a reason! You are priceless!
2. Go outside and enjoy nature. Take a walk!
3. Get a journal book: Make a list of things you are good at and what you are thankful for. Then each day, write down a new blessing, something good. Read this when you are feeling doubtful.
4. Build positive relationships and stay away from negative people as they will only bring you down.
5. Realize it is good and okay to say "no!"
6. Don't watch or listen to anything negative (for example, the news..
7. Be positive and be kind to yourself and others!
8. Realize we all make mistakes, and none of us are perfect; it is okay!
9. Do what you love or have compassion for.

I know I have always chosen the non-typical paths; I have heard how crazy I was. I used to get upset, but now I just laugh. I have accepted it. I have confidence in my abilities and myself. It is my journey in life, and I choose to surround myself with positive people and to help inspire courage and confidence in others. My challenge to you is that I want you to inspire confidence in a friend or someone you do not know. (Just a simple smile or "thank you" is a start.)

Go to my website for a bonus worksheet:
www.powerofartandnature.com.

Finding Yourself

Finding yourself is an essential step in finding out who you really are. At various stages of life, we need to ask who we are, as sometimes we get so busy that we forget. So let us take the time to find ourselves. The first time in life when we need to ask ourselves the following questions is as a teenager. I just want to express that you should never do something you think somebody else wants you to do because they believe you would be good at it, that you should do what they do, or because it pays well. It takes bravery and courage to do what you love. Sometimes in life, we forget about living a life filled with joy and, instead, take on jobs that we hate and live where we do not want to. It is like this: It is not about the money. Realize that money is just a tool to live the lifestyle you want to live. Life is too short to do what you hate.

Here are some questions you need to ask yourself. But, of course, there is no right or wrong answer, and you may have several answers for each question.

1. What is it that you enjoy?
2. What would you do for free that you enjoy?
3. Do you have specific skills or hobbies that you love?
4. What do people tell you that you are good at?
5. Where do you like working, inside or outside?
6. Do you like creating on a computer or in a shop?
7. Do you like working with your hands or sitting at a desk?
8. Do you like working with people?
9. Do you want to set your own hours, or do you like someone setting your schedule?
10. Do you like working for others?
11. What is more important to you, security or freedom?
12. What are the most important things to you in life?
13. What are your values? (Example: positivity, communication, fun)
14. Where do you want to live? If you had a family, where would you want to live?
15. Have you ever volunteered or done something you enjoyed for someone else?
16. What would you do if you did not need anything, including money?

Thanks for being brave. Now let's look at your answers. Have you noticed anything? I hope you learned more about yourself and what you enjoy in life by answering these questions. Now let us see if you have a hidden talent.

**Go to my website for a bonus worksheet:
www.powerofartandnature.com.**

Talent or Gift?

Identifying your talent or gift can be both a fun and rewarding process. To get started, think about the things you love and are passionate about. What are you naturally good at? What do other people tell you that you're good at? Once you have a few ideas in mind, start exploring them further. If you are interested in painting, for example, try attending a class or workshop. Or if you enjoy writing, start working on a book or blog. The more you explore your talent or gift, the more it will begin to take shape. And before long, you will have a better understanding of what makes you unique.

When I think about talent, I often think about things like singing, dancing, or playing instruments. However, talent comes in many different forms. For example, you are good at a particular sport, or you have a unique talent for speaking or video editing. Whatever your talent may be, it's important to remember that it is a gift that makes you unique. You can use your talent to pursue a career in the arts or athletics, or you can use it to find a job that you love. Ultimately, your talent is something that you can use to make your life more enjoyable and fulfilling. So do not be afraid to pursue your passions and use your talents to their fullest potential.

Even the greatest artists did not become who they are overnight. They all had to start somewhere, and most of them went through a phase of finding their own style. If you're just starting out, it is important to experiment with different techniques and styles until you find something that feels natural to you. It's also important to be patient; talent and creativity take time to develop. Just keep exploring and pushing yourself, and eventually you will find your own unique voice as an artist. And once you do, you will be able to take your work to a whole new level.

Finding Your Style

It is often said that talent is only half the battle when it comes to being a successful artist—the other half is finding your own style. And it's true, to a certain extent. After all, there are countless gifted artists out there who never quite find their niche and, as a result, never reach the level of success they crave. But why is this? Why is it that some artists find their style quite easily while others struggle for years with no end in sight?

There are a few possible explanations. Firstly, it could be argued that talent does indeed play a role. Perhaps those artists who find their style quickly are simply more talented than those who do not. They have a natural gift for art that allows them to experiment and play around until they eventually stumble upon a style that feels right. On the other hand, it could be argued that talent has nothing to do with it; that finding your own style is simply a matter of trial and error. Eventually, everyone finds something that works for them.

Whatever the explanation may be, one thing is for sure: If you want to take your art or talent to the next level, you must find your own style. It might take weeks, months, or even years, but eventually, you will get there; and when you do, you will be glad you did.

Talent is a gift that I believe everyone has. It is just a matter of uncovering it and developing it. For me, finding my style was a process of trial and error. I tried out different mediums and techniques and studied other artists to see how they did things. Slowly but surely, I began to develop my own style. And while I made plenty of mistakes along the way, I never gave up. In the end, my persistence paid off and I discovered my true style.

All my life, I have been creative. It is a gift that I was born with, and it is something that I cherish. I express myself through art, and it is a way for me to connect with the world around me. When I create something, I pour my heart and soul into it. That way, my art will truly reflect who I am. And hopefully, it will inspire others to be creative and express themselves in their own unique way.

We all have something special to offer, and creativity is one of the most powerful tools. We must share our gifts with the world. So let us all strive to be a little more creative every day and make the world a more beautiful place in the process.

Embrace Your Uniqueness

First, realize it is okay to be different. Each one of us has gone through different things in life that others haven't. We have lived with, learned, or been challenged by various things we have encountered. This has given us life skills that others have not experienced. We have all traveled to various places, lived in different areas, or been surrounded by different things and types of people. It is what makes us who we are. Our talent is a gift that makes us unique and defines us as individuals. When we accept this about ourselves, we can use our talent to succeed and be happy in whatever we choose to do in life. Being different is what makes us special. So, embrace it and let your talent shine!

It is a talent to be able to listen to people, to hear what they are saying and to understand their needs. It is a gift to be able to encourage people, to build them up and help them achieve their dreams. Sadly, most people do not have this talent or gift. They question our motives, values, and talents. They put doubt in our minds, even if it is not intentional. As a result, we doubt ourselves and our abilities. We question our talent and whether we are good enough. We doubt our value and worth. We may even give up on our dreams because of the doubt that has been placed in our minds. However, we must never give up on ourselves. We must never give up on our dreams. We must never let the doubters win. Instead, we must use our talents and gifts to encourage and inspire others. And in doing so, we will find the strength to overcome the doubt and achieve our own dreams.

We all have something that makes us unique. It might be a talent or skill that we have, or a certain way of thinking or feeling. Whatever it is, it is what makes us special and sets us apart from everyone else. And that is something to be embraced, not hidden away.

Too often, people try to blend in and conform to what they think is the norm. But what they do not realize is that by doing so, they are losing what makes them special. They become just another face in the crowd. But when you embrace your uniqueness, you stand out from the rest. You are individuals who are talented and gifted in your own ways. And that is something to be celebrated, not hidden away.

So do not be afraid to show the world who you really are. Embrace your uniqueness and let your talent and gifts shine through. You will be surprised at how far it takes you in life.

As an artist, I am always striving to create something new and unique. I love the feeling of taking a blank canvas and turning it into something beautiful. It is like bringing something to life. Each painting or sculpture becomes an original work with its own story to tell, which makes it all worthwhile for me! My talent is my gift, and I strive to use it to inspire others. I hope that my art will touch people in a way that they never thought possible.

In a world where it feels like everyone is trying to be the same, it is more important than ever to find ways to stand out. We all have unique talents and gifts that make us special. It's our job to find ways to use those talents to stand out from the crowd. There are so many ways to be creative and get noticed. Whether it is through our art, writing, fashion, or the way we carry ourselves, we need to find ways to express our uniqueness. When we do, we will be surprised at how many people we inspire along the way. So let us get creative and find our own unique way to stand out from the crowd.

Gene's Multnomah Falls

Chapter 5
Creativeness

5

Discovery

There are many benefits to being brave. First, you'll have increased self-confidence, making life more fun! Your creativity will flow much easier when you're not worried about what could go wrong or be embarrassing for everyone around us, because there's no fear at all.

The discovery of your courage and inner creativeness is a step into discovering how unique each person is.

What is courage? "Courage is the choice and willingness to confront agony, pain, danger, uncertainty, or intimidation..." (Wikipedia)

Think of it this way: Taking action despite our fears is courage. Likewise, taking a leap into the unknown with no guarantees of success is courage.

Inspiration is the key to creativeness, and courage is the key to inspiration. A person without courage has already given up on themselves before they even start challenging or discovering themselves creatively. Creative expression comes naturally when one does not worry about other people's thoughts. Inspiration is all around us; we just have to be brave enough to see it.

It takes courage to tell somebody what you think, to trust others, or try new things. It takes courage to say no, to admit when we are wrong, or to say I am sorry. Yet, for some, it takes courage just to get out of bed in the morning, go to school, start or quit a job, or start their own business. Why is that? It is the fear of the unknown. We must be brave and daring every day. There is no room for fear in life because it will only hold us back from achieving our dreams or goals that often could lead to accomplishments that make others proud of us too! So go out there and be brave! Take some risks! Inspire others with your creativity! Let your courage shine through!

One way I have found when facing a new challenge is to make 2 lists. What are the positive things, and what are the negative things? When I know the worst thing, I can then decide whether to proceed or not with my decision. Here is an example: When I paint a wall, I will either like the color or not. If I do not like the color, the worst thing would be that I would have to repaint. Therefore, I will paint my wall.

Many people go through life without ever really testing their limits. Instead, they stick to the familiar and the comfortable, never straying too far from the beaten path. But what if you could discover joy and creativity by taking on a new challenge? What if you found the courage and creativeness needed to succeed?

It is worth taking the time to find out. By exploring new territory, you open yourself up to new possibilities. You might just surprise yourself with what you are capable of. So go ahead and take that first step into the unknown. It could be the beginning of a beautiful journey.

Any artist will tell you that the creative process is often fraught with doubts and fears. But unfortunately, uncertainty is simply part of the territory. So, when I take on a new project, especially one as large and complex as a giant 3-D wall sculpture, I am a little nervous at first. But that is precisely what I enjoy about the creative process—the sense of discovery, and the joy of pushing myself to do something that I may have thought was beyond my abilities. All those doubts and fears vanish when a piece is finished and installed, and they are replaced by a sense of pride and accomplishment. To me, that is the true joy of being an artist.

For me, the garden has always been a place of inspiration and creative discovery. There is always something new to discover. A garden is a place where I can be creative and express my love for the outdoors. There is something therapeutic about being out in nature, surrounded by the beauty of plants and flowers.

Therapy in the Garden

I always find natural therapy in my garden or nature when I take the time to sit, watch, and listen. I believe everyone should spend more time outside in nature, instead of noticing all our problems, aches, and pains. Rather, see the beautiful flowers, plants, trees, birds, butterflies, and bees. Have you ever just sat and watched a moose meander, robins build a nest, or a chipmunk check out grapes to see if they are ready to eat? These are a few of the things I have been able to experience quite often, living where we do. Nature can be the best therapist.

Another example: Today, when I walked out onto my front porch to water my hanging basket, I looked down in the yard, and it looked like I was on the movie set of *Bambi*—wild turkeys with babies, a bunny, deer in the yard, and a robin taking a bath in the stream. This is all so inspiring. I sat down in my garden to just take it all in. As I sat there, I felt my body relax, and all my worries faded. This is what I like to call therapy in the garden.

Being surrounded by nature and all its beauty puts things into perspective and reminds us of what is truly important in life. If you ever feel stressed, hurt, or overwhelmed, I encourage you to take a walk in nature or spend some time tending to your garden. It is amazing how much peace and comfort can be found in the simple act of surrounding yourself with living things. You will be surprised at how much better you will feel afterward.

The sound of water trickling down a garden fountain can be incredibly calming, while the sight of a vast ocean can fill us with a sense of awe. In fact, spending time near water has been shown to reduce stress levels and promote feelings of well-being. For many people, simply being in the presence of water is enough to inspire creativity and feelings of peace. In these ways, water can act as a powerful form of therapy, offering us a chance to relax and recharge.

River in Glacier

Water Is Soothing to the Soul

Have you ever noticed how water is soothing to the soul? The gentle sounds of trickling water can be very Inspiring, and sometimes all it takes is a little water to help get those creative juices flowing. Maybe you like the sound of soft waves on a lake shoreline, or the gentle tumble of water cascading down a mountainside. Do you prefer the exhilarating sounds of ocean waves hitting the cliffs during a thunderstorm, or roaring waterfalls? Either way, there is no denying that water has a way of Inspiring us. That is why so many talented artists and writers have gardens with water features. There is just something about being surrounded by the gentle sounds of water that helps to stimulate creativity. So next time you feel stuck, try spending some time near a body of water. You might find it is precisely what you need to get those creative juices flowing again.

Our family loves the water. Whenever we go on vacation or a weekend outing, we always go to a water destination. We like hiking to waterfalls or hidden lakes, and boating, swimming, and fishing on one of the many lakes in our beautiful area. Of course, we always enjoy going to the ocean, where there is always plenty to explore. The water is inspiring and a beautiful place to get away from everything and just relax. We like to fish, swim, and just enjoy sitting on the shore and listening to the sound of the waves crashing against the rocks. It is very soothing to the soul. Something about the water is very inspiring, and it helps me to be more artistic in my garden design and art.

Inspiration can come from many places. For some, it is the sight of a beautiful garden that sparks creativity. For others, it is the sound of a babbling brook that leads to a sense of tranquility. And for others still, it is the gentle flow of a waterfall that brings a sense of peace. No matter what inspires you, there is no doubt that water is soothing to the soul. By adding a small pond or stream to your landscape, you can create a beautiful and serene space. Whether you choose to do it yourself or have it done for you, the result will be an oasis you can enjoy for years to come.

I have always been inspired by nature, and I especially love the sights and sounds of water. Water captivates the senses, whether it is a babbling brook or a crashing wave, and I always include a lake or stream in my paintings and sculptures. When you look at one of my pieces, I want you to be transported to that place—standing next to the stream, watching the sunset over the lake, or feeling the mist of the waves. I hope that by bringing nature inside, we can all find a little peace and tranquility in our busy lives.

Art Lessons

Inspiration can come from anywhere. For me, I am constantly inspired by the world around me. Whether it is the way the sun hits the water or the way a flower is drawn, I think that art should always be fun. If you do not enjoy what you are creating, it shows in the finished product. When I take an art lesson, I always try to paint or draw something that I would hang in my house—something that has meaning to me. What about you? What inspires you? Do you take art lessons? I think everyone could benefit from a little creativity in their lives!

Inspiration can come from anywhere: from the colors and shapes in nature, to the people we interact with daily. When it comes to art, there are no right or wrong answers; only the opportunity to explore different techniques and mediums and have fun. I tend to take my art a little more seriously than most, but that does not mean I do not enjoy creating and painting. On the contrary, I love looking for inspiration in the world around me, whether it is the different shades of green on every leaf or the changing colors of the sky at sunset. Art is a way to express ourselves and connect with the world around us. I believe that everyone has the potential to be creative.

Art has the ability to inspire creativity and help people to see the world in new ways. It can also be a form of self-expression, allowing people to share their unique perspectives with the world. For many people, art is also a way to relieve stress and escape life's daily pressures. In an art lesson, students can momentarily relax and live in the moment without any outside distractions. Whether it is painting, sculpture, or pottery, art provides a creative outlet that can help to reduce stress and promote positive mental health. So next time you feel overwhelmed, consider signing up for an art class. It might just be the thing you need to help you relax and find your inner artist.

Inspiration can come from anywhere. For artists, it is often found in the world around them. To truly capture the world around them, artists must be willing to look at it with fresh eyes. They must be willing to see the beauty in the everyday and the extraordinary. This can be a challenge, but it is also what makes art so special. It is what allows us to see the world in new and exciting ways.

"This I learned from the shadow of a tree. ..our influence may fall where we can never be."

author unknown

Shadow of a Tree

Drawing What You See

The world is a beautiful place, and there is so much to see. However, we often take for granted the sights that are right in front of us. To truly see the world, we must open our eyes and look around. Inspiration can be found anywhere, and it is up to us to find it. One way to do this is through art. By observing the world around us and recreating it in our own way, we can gain a new perspective on familiar sights. This can be done through any medium, whether it be painting, pottery, glass blowing, or even just drawing in a sketchbook. The important thing is to take the time to really see what is around us. The world is full of beauty, and it is waiting for us to discover it.

When you come to my studio for an art lesson, the first thing I will have you do is walk around my yard and take in your surroundings. I want you to notice the color of the sky, the green grass, the forest that surrounds us, the flowers, the plants, and bushes, and listen to the trickling of the streams.

Take a close look at the trees—you will notice cedars, fir, pine, aspen, birches, and a few other varieties. Now we will focus on one tree. I want you to focus on an aspen. You will notice, at the tree's base, that the roots go down into the soil. Trees start in the ground. As we start moving up the tree, you will notice the bark. Is it smooth or rough, and are there any markings on the bark, like from a young buck rubbing his antlers on the tree? Then, extend your gaze up to the leaves and branches. Notice how the leaves quiver in the slightest breeze.

I want you to take all of this in and use it as inspiration for your next painting or piece of art. Creativity comes from all around us; we must be open to seeing it. Who knows, this walk may inspire your next masterpiece. We can learn a lot from a tree.

Go to my website for a bonus worksheet:
www.powerofartandnature.com.

Endless Possibilities

Inspiration can come from anywhere—a song, a color, a smell, a memory. The artist's job is to take that inspiration and turn it into something tangible—a painting, a sculpture, a building, or even just an arrangement of flowers. The possibilities are truly endless. And while some people are naturally more creative than others, creativity is something that can be cultivated. Like a muscle, the more you use it, the stronger it becomes. If you allow yourself to be open to new ideas and new ways of seeing the world, you will find that your creativity will begin to flow. There are also many ways to create an environment conducive to creativity, such as surrounding yourself with inspiring objects, making time for quiet reflection, or simply opening your mind to the possibility of magic.

When it comes to design, your home is your canvas, and you are the artist. The world is your oyster when it comes to inspiration—there is no limit to what you can do. And when it comes to color, warm tones are always welcoming and inviting. You will find that these colors are relaxing and will decrease anxiety. In fact, hospitals often paint the children's and maternity areas in warm tones for this very reason. So, carry the colors throughout your home for a cohesive look. A pop of color here and there can really brighten things up and add interest. But when your home flows with a welcoming energy, you will find that endless possibilities await you. Let your creativity shine and enjoy the process. It is your home—make it exactly what you want it to be.

I love bringing the outdoors inside! When I am working with clients, I really take the time to listen to them and get to know them. I want to understand their design aesthetic and what colors they are drawn to. With that information, I can create a 3D wall sculpture that perfectly fits their personality and home. It is so rewarding to see the look of excitement on their face when they see the finished product for the first time! For me, art is all about endless possibilities and reflecting the imagination. Everyone has an artist within them just waiting to be unleashed! So, when my clients commission me to create a piece for them, I am helping them bring their own inner artist out into the light. It is such an honor to be able to do that!

Let us check the possibilities outside: When you walk outside, does your outdoor area flow with the inside of your home? Inspiration for your outdoor area can come from many places. Maybe you saw a photo in a magazine or visited a friend's home and loved their landscape. Wherever you find your inspiration, remember that your outdoor area should be an extension of your indoor living space. Just as you put thought into furnishing and decorating your rooms, so too should you approach your outdoor area. With a little creativity, the possibilities are endless. Consider furniture placement, lighting, and even planting trees or flowers to create a cohesive space that you and your family will love spending time in.

It is important to remember that time is precious and that we only have a limited amount of it. So, it is worth considering how we can make the most of it. There are endless possibilities available to us if we only take the time to imagine them.

Sunset Surrender

Chapter 6
Time

6

Take Time to Appreciate

nspiration is everywhere—the sunbeam that spills across your bed in the morning, or the way the leaves rustle in the wind. It is in a smile from a stranger, in a kind word from a friend. Inspiration is all around us, but sometimes we need to take the time to appreciate it.

We need to slow down and take the time to appreciate everything, both big and small. When we do this, life becomes more vibrant and more exciting. We start to see all the little things that make life so unique.

Take some time today to appreciate everything around you. Everything that makes up your life is your family, friends, home, and world. It really is a beautiful place.

Too often, we take for granted the things that bring us joy. We can miss a beautiful sunset because we are too busy working or scrolling through our phones. We can fail to appreciate a child's laughter because we are wrapped up in our lives. But each moment is fleeting, and before we know it, they are gone.

Have you ever thought about how important it is to take the time to show our gratitude for the people and things we love? When a person gives up their time to be with us, it is a very precious gift. They could be spending their time elsewhere but have chosen to spend it with us instead. Or when somebody uses their money to buy us a gift, they are sacrificing their own desires to make us happy. When someone makes something special for us, they are taking the time and effort to create something just for us, out of their own joy and appreciation.

Gratitude is one of the most important emotions we can feel because it helps us to connect with the things that truly matter in life. It fills us with joy and appreciation and reminds us of how lucky we are. So next time you are grateful, take a moment to tell the people and things you love just how much you appreciate them. It will make all the difference in the world!

So let us all be thankful for what we have and show appreciation for the gift life offers. Let us also be grateful for the chance to experience all this world has to offer. Finally, let us be thankful for each other and, most importantly, be grateful for God's gift of life. Life is a beautiful thing—let us not take it for granted!

Time vs. Time

How do we spend our time? What does that say about us? Do we spend our time wisely? Or do we let time slip through our fingers?

It is an interesting concept, this idea of time vs. time. How do we spend our time? Are we taking the time to work on a project or are we taking time to spend with family and friends? What is the quality of the time that we are spending? Is it meaningful and productive? Or is it just filling up space?

It is important to consider how we spend our time because it can reflect who we are as people. If we are constantly running around trying to fit everything in, we might not be able to enjoy the moment. We might not be able to appreciate the power of art or nature. We might not be able to connect with people on a deeper level.

So maybe it's worth taking some time to think about how we want to spend our time. It is worth making more of an effort to connect with people and experiences that inspire us. It's worth marveling at the world around us and all the beauty that it has to offer. After all, life is too short to let time slip away without savoring it first.

Time is a precious commodity. We each have the same amount of time each day, so we need to be wise about how we spend it.

Minutes Turn to Hours

If we are not careful, seconds turn into minutes, minutes turn into hours, and hours turn into days. So, think about this: There are 60 seconds in one minute, 60 minutes in an hour, 24 hours in a day, 7 days in a week, and 365 days (about 12 months) in a year.

So how are you spending your time?

Think about this: Spending 1 day a month having dinner with family is only 12 times a year. If you only spend the major holidays with family, that is even less, like 3? If your family or friends are essential, you may want to prioritize them.

How many hours a day are you constantly on your phone or looking at a computer screen? Most think it is only a few minutes. Still, it is more than you think; it is an addiction for some. Are you so busy going from one sports event or lesson to another, that you have not been available to enjoy life or others?

What if we took the time to spend 30 minutes each day outside? Instead of looking at our phones or TV, we look at nature. How would that change the way we feel? The way we interact with others? We often forget how fulfilling it can be to simply be present in the moment and appreciate the beauty surrounding us.

When we are caught up in the hustle and bustle of everyday life, it is essential to take a step back and remember what is profoundly important. That is why it is vital to find ways to slow down and enjoy the little things in life.

Whether taking a leisurely walk through the park or taking a moment to admire a sunset, taking the time to appreciate the simple things can make all the difference. At times, we need extra time just to recharge. After all, life is meant to be enjoyed, not simply endured.

Take That Vacation

Vacation—what is the first thing that comes to your mind when you hear that word? For some people, it may be lying on a beach with a tropical drink in hand. Others may think of hiking through nature and enjoying the fresh air. No matter your idea of a vacation, there are many benefits to taking some time off from work or school and exploring the world around you. Vacations allow you to relax and rejuvenate, spend time with loved ones, see unfamiliar places, and experience new things. They also offer an opportunity to appreciate the natural world and the power of nature. So, if you are feeling stressed or burned out, it is time to take that vacation.

Vacations are an important investment in our health. They give us time to relax and recharge away from the hustle and bustle of everyday life. One of the most important aspects of a vacation is experiencing new things and using all our senses. For me, it means sitting around a campfire, listening to the crackling of the fire, and feeling the warmth on my skin. It means kayaking in the ocean, feeling the mist created by the waves, and smelling the salty sea air. It means taking in nature's beauty and realizing its power to calm and refresh our minds and bodies.

Virtual vacations may be a convenient way to take a break, but they can never replace the real thing. So, if you are feeling stressed or burned out, maybe it's time to take that real vacation—some "me" time.

Dahlia

Take Time for You

We live in a fast-paced world where it is easy to get caught up in the hustle and bustle of everyday life. Sometimes we can be so busy that we forget it is important to take time for ourselves. Remember that taking time out for yourself is not selfish—it's crucial for maintaining your mental and physical health.

There are myriad ways to take time for yourself, but one of the most effective is through art. Art has the power to transport us to another world entirely, where we can forget our troubles and simply exist in the moment. Whether it is painting, drawing, sculpting, or just appreciating art, spending time surrounded by beauty can help to center and calm us.

Nature also has the power to rejuvenate and refresh us. Immersing ourselves in nature—whether it is taking a hike in the woods or simply spending time in our own backyard—can help to ground us and remind us of what truly matters in life. When we take the time to connect with nature, we give ourselves permission to slow down and just be.

So next time you feel overwhelmed, take a few minutes (or even an hour) for yourself. Turn off your phone, step away from your work, and allow yourself to experience the healing power of art and nature. Your body—and your mind—will thank you for it.

Stop. Breathe in. Do you smell that? It is the smell of roses; sweet, heady, and romantic. But what does it really mean to slow down and appreciate life? For some, it may simply mean taking a moment to appreciate the little things in life. However, for others, it may be a reminder that tomorrow is not guaranteed.

Live as If it's Your Last Day

Today could be your last day on Earth. How would you spend it? Would you spend it with your family, friends, or loved ones? Would you travel to a place you have always wanted to see, or would you stay home and reflect on your life? No matter how you spend your final day, making the most of it is essential. After all, we only have a limited time on this Earth. By being mindful of how we spend our time, we can ensure that we live life to the fullest.

Art can inspire us and help us see the world in new ways. It can also help us connect with our emotions and express ourselves creatively. The power of art is that it can connect us to something larger than ourselves. It can remind us of nature's beauty and time's preciousness. Art can help us see the world through new eyes and appreciate it in all its forms.

Another way to make the most of your time is to spend time in nature. Nature has a way of grounding us and helping us appreciate the beauty of life. We can marvel at the power of thunderstorms, the majesty of mountains, and the tranquil beauty of a gentle stream. It is a gentle reminder that everything is temporary and that we should cherish every moment.

Whatever you do today, make sure to savor every moment. Live each day as if it's your last. Surround yourself with those things that make you feel alive, those things that make you feel happy, and those things that inspire you. Because when you do, life will be more beautiful than ever imagined.

Pine Creek

Chapter 7
Positivity

7

Surround Yourself

Have you ever stopped to think about the people who surround you daily? The ones who you confide in, share your triumphs and struggles with, and who support you no matter what? These are the people who make up your inner circle, and they play a crucial role in your overall well-being. Research has shown that surrounding yourself with positive people who bring out the best in you can help to improve your outlook on life. In addition, it will increase your sense of happiness and fulfillment. So next time you are feeling low, take a step back and assess the people in your life.

If you are surrounded by negativity, make a conscious effort to spend more time in nature, engage with art, and seek out positive relationships; that will inspire and support you. Spending time in nature has been shown to reduce stress levels, improve moods, and boost overall health. It is a wonderful way to center yourself and recharge your batteries. Engaging with art, whether through painting, sculpture, or simply admiring beautiful works of art, can also help uplift your spirits and remind you of the beauty in the world. And finally, seeking out positive relationships will fill your life with warmth, positivity, and joy. So do not be afraid to reach out to those who make you feel good—they just might be the key to improving your overall well-being.

We are often unaware of the effect that our surroundings have on us. The sights and smells of our environment can trigger certain memories or moods, for better or for worse. The music we listen to, the books we read, and the people we surround ourselves with also influence our moods and emotions.

What Are You Listening To?

We are constantly bombarded with noise. Day in and day out, we hear the sound of traffic, of people talking, and of TVs and radios blaring. It can be easy to tune all of this out and simply exist in a state of white noise. But what we listen to in our surroundings can also affect us. Therefore, it can be essential to surround yourself with positive sounds.

The chirping of birds, the rustling of leaves in the wind, and the sound of waves crashing against the shore are all sounds that can fill us with a sense of peace and calm. When we take the time to truly listen to the world around us, we can find beauty and inspiration in even the simplest of sounds.

We often think of our taste in music as a personal preference, but the truth is that what we listen to can profoundly affect our mood and state of mind. Studies have shown that music with a slow tempo and soothing lyrics can help to lower stress levels. In contrast, upbeat music can improve our energy and motivation. In addition, the type of music we listen to can also affect our level of creativity.

Suppose we surround ourselves with positive and inspiring music. In that case, we are more likely to be in a creative and productive state of mind. On the other hand, if we constantly listen to angry or depressing music, it can negatively affect our mood and thoughts. Therefore, it is crucial to be mindful of the type of music we allow into our lives, as it can significantly impact our well-being.

So, if you are looking to boost your mood or reduce stress, surround yourself with positive influences. That includes spending more time outside, listening to soothing music, looking at or creating art, or hanging out with upbeat friends. By filling your life with good vibes, you will start to feel better in no time.

Seeing

Art and nature have always been intertwined. For centuries, artists have been inspired by the beauty of the natural world; they have used their art to try to capture its essence. In turn, art has the power to inspire and change the way we see the world. When we look at a beautiful painting or sculpture, we are reminded of the potential for beauty and harmony in our lives. Art can also be found in unexpected places, such as in the art of a child's drawing or patterns formed by clouds in the sky. Even something as simple as a bunch of flowers can remind us of the natural world and its ability to bring joy into our lives.

Similarly, nature has its own unique way of speaking to us. The beauty of a sunset, the peace of a forest, and the majesty of a mountain are all powerful to fill us with wonder and awe. When we are surrounded by art and nature, it is easier to see the world in a positive light. We are reminded of the beauty and mystery of life, and we are given a renewed sense of hope and possibility. Art and nature have the power to change our mindsets and our world.

As I see the world, I see it as a positive place. So many good things happen every day, and I feel fortunate to be alive and able to experience them. From the beauty of a sunset to a child's laughter, there is so much good in the world.

It is easy to get caught up in the negative aspects of life, but if you take the time to look around, you will see that there is so much to be grateful for. Make an effort to focus on the positive things in your life, and you will be amazed at how much happier you will become.

Negativity vs. Positivity

Some people may think the glass is half empty, while others may see it as half full. The truth is that the glass is refillable. This comparison between a negative vs. positive outlook can be applied to everyday life. It is how an individual views the world around them—their perspective.

People with a positive attitude will pay attention to the good rather than the bad in people, situations, and events. By seeing the positive, they are more likely to have a positive outlook on life, which can lead to a happier and more prosperous future. Additionally, individuals who surround themselves with positivity are more likely to have a positive attitude. On the other hand, those who choose to see the negative may miss out on opportunities and experiences because they are bogged down by negativity.

Every day, we are faced with a choice. We can focus on the negative aspects of our lives and allow those to bring us down, or we can choose to see the positive and let that inspire us. Finding the silver lining may not always be easy, but it is always worth the effort. After all, a positive attitude can lead to better health, improved relationships, and increased success in all areas of life. So, the next time you feel down, take a moment to appreciate the beauty of nature, the joy of seeing a loved one smile, or the satisfaction of completing a task. These small moments of positivity will remind you of the power of choice and help you maintain a positive outlook on life.

Art has a way of reminding us of the essential things in life. It can help us see nature's beauty and inspire us to be more positive. Art can also remind us of our potential and help us see the world in new ways. Whenever we feel lost or uncertain, art can be a powerful reminder of who we are and what we are capable of.

Golden Eagle Falls

Art Tells a Story

Art has a way of capturing the beauty of nature and the joy of seeing the world through new eyes. It can inspire us to be positive and grateful for what we have. Art can take many forms, from painting and sculpture to poetry and dance. Each type of art has its own unique ability to tell a story. Whether it is a story about the artist's life or about the world around us, art has the power to inspire and enlighten.

I love getting to know my clients and hearing their stories. It helps me to understand their style and what they are looking for in a piece of art. I ask to see photos of their home, art, and other places unique to them. I take note of the colors they are drawn to and the overall style of their home. This gives me a good starting point for creating a custom piece of art that they will love. I often sketch out a potential design based on our conversation and what they are looking for.

When we meet again, I show them the artist's rendering and how it would look in their home or business. My job as an artist is to visualize what they want to be created and bring it to life through my artwork.

Here is an example of a commission: When I met up with one of my favorite clients, Sonja and David, at their home, I asked them which one of the pieces of my art really spoke to them. It was "Stillness in the Reeds," a 3-D oil sculpture of a heron. Sonja wanted the piece I was creating for them to be in the same color tones: the trees to be the same type as what they had outside, and the water to look natural.

This piece we created would be installed in a stairway entryway in their home. It would be a statement piece (4 ft. by 14 ft.).

I love creating art that tells a story. And that is precisely what I did with my 3D wall sculpture, "Golden Eagle Falls." The husband, David, told me some incredible hiking stories of different trails he had been on, including one where he saw golden eagles flying overhead. As luck would have it, I had just taken photos of two golden eagles soaring above us a few days earlier, so I knew those would fit perfectly into the scene. So, after drawing up the sketches and getting approval, I created the 3D wall sculpture. It was like a giant puzzle, as it was created on five different panels that were installed, and the seams were filled in so that it would look like one piece. Then, it was finished on-site.

Every time my clients or I look at it, it feels like we are transported to that magical place where eagles soar and waterfalls cascade. It is a reminder of nature's beauty and wonder and the power of art to inspire and reflect. This 3D wall sculpture is one of my favorite masterpieces because it tells a story and reminds those who see it that they helped create it.

A well-chosen piece of art can brighten up a room and make it feel more inviting. It can also have a calming effect, helping to create a positive environment. The wall sculpture in this home is a perfect example of this.

It is not only a representation of the artist's creative power but also a reminder of the natural world. The wall sculpture reminds us that art can be used to inspire and heal. It is a reminder that the power of art is immense. The wall sculpture is a beautiful art that all can enjoy, just like plants in nature.

Plants Need a Positive Environment

The power of nature is undeniable. Just look at how plants can thrive in even the most adverse conditions. They are a reminder that anything is possible with the right environment. When it comes to growth and development, plants need light, temperature, water, and humidity. But they also need something else: love. That's right; plants need a positive environment to really flourish. And what better place to provide that than in your home or office? By keeping plants indoors, you can create a peaceful and calm interior. Plus, you will get to enjoy the beauty of nature every day. So do not wait any longer. Give your plants the love they need and watch them grow!

The world is a canvas, and nature is the paint. So often, we get caught up in the mundane and forget to appreciate the simple beauty around us. Plant power can help us see the world in a new light. They provide us with a sense of joy and peace that can be hard to find in our fast-paced lives. Surrounding ourselves with plants can help to create a positive environment that supports our well-being. It is time to let nature back into our lives and experience the beauty of the world around us.

Plants have always been a natural element in a positive environment. The power of nature is unexplainable; it just has this ability to make us feel good. Plants bring joy and happiness; they are antidotes to sadness and stress. We create a calm, serene, and beautiful space when we surround ourselves with plants.

Mountain Views

Chapter 8
Fun

8

Finding Daily Joy

There is something special about waking up to a new day. No matter what yesterday brought, today is a fresh start. As the sun rises, it is a reminder that nature is always moving forward. And we can too.

We can find daily joy in even the simplest things by taking a moment to appreciate what we have. Whether watching the sunrise, enjoying a cup of coffee, or taking a nature walk, savoring the moment can help us feel more connected and alive. When we take the time to do things we enjoy, we open ourselves up to happiness and possibility. Finding daily joy is easy when you let yourself be open to the possibilities.

There is something special about the simple joys in life. It is the way they make us feel connected to nature or the fact that they remind us of the power of nature to inspire happiness.

For this reason, enjoying activities that make us happy is integral to finding daily joy, whether playing with our kids, going for a walk in the park, or simply taking a few moments to admire the sunset. It is a joy to share these things with others and see the joy on their faces too. When we take the time to enjoy these simple joys, we open our hearts to compassion and happiness.

One of the best ways to find joy is to bless others with our time and talents. When we focus on improving someone else's life, we often find that our lives are enhanced. So, making time for things that bring us happiness can go a long way toward brightening our day-to-day lives.

So let yourself have some fun every day—it is good for your soul! You never know when a little bit of joy will make all the difference and bless you simultaneously.

Be available for activities that make you smile. Finally, remember that joy can be found in the everyday moments of life. It may not be flashy or exciting, but it is always there waiting for us if we take the time to notice it.

Blessed

Blessed are those who enjoy life and see positivity and blessings around us. Their hearts and homes are filled with joy, and they bring joy to others. They find fun in the simple things of life. They are happy with what today has to offer them. They do not need much because nature has already provided them with everything they need. All they need is a good attitude, a smile, and the willingness to have fun.

You cannot help but feel happy when you are around them. There is just something about their positive energy that is contagious. It is like they have found the secret to happiness, and they are sharing it with the world. We could all learn something from them about enjoying life and seeing the beauty in everything around us.

Remember, one of the most powerful blessings in life is nature. Nature has the power to refresh and renew us. When we are surrounded by nature, we can feel its healing presence. We can also enjoy nature, playing games, hiking, swimming, and exploring. Being in nature fills us with joy and a sense of wonder.

One of the best things in life is being able to bless others with your happiness. When you are happiest and most positive, you naturally want to spread that feeling to those around you. It is as if your inner joy is overflowing and spilling out into the world around you, touching everyone it interacts with. This is one of the most unique gifts you can give others.

When you are truly joyful, you inspire those around you to be happier and more positive. You become a source of light and happiness in their lives, which is truly remarkable. So blessed be those who can share their joy with the world! They are indeed a blessing to everyone they meet.

Lily Sunrise

Pursue What You Enjoy

What is it that you enjoy? What brings you happiness and satisfaction? These are essential questions to ask yourself because your answer can provide you with the motivation to pursue your dreams. It can be easy to get caught up in the mundane tasks of everyday life. Still, if we take the time to appreciate the things that bring us joy, we can find the inspiration to pursue our passions.

For me, nature is one of the most significant sources of Joy. There is something about being in nature that just makes me feel good. The fresh air, the beauty of the scenery, and the sense of peace and tranquility I feel when surrounded by nature is simply unparalleled. When I am in nature, I am reminded of how lucky I am to be alive and experience these things. This gratitude inspires me to pursue my dreams and continue doing the things I enjoy.

So, whatever brings you joy, make sure you pursue it! Life is too short to waste time doing things we do not enjoy. Instead, seek out opportunities to do the things you love and value! Pursuing what we enjoy is one of the best ways to guarantee a happy and fulfilling life.

I enjoy doing things that are fun and make me laugh. Life is too short to be serious all the time, so I try to enjoy the lighter moments as much as possible. Pursuing what you enjoy is essential to living a happy and fulfilling life. We all have our passions and talents, so it is important to find what makes us happy and pursue it with everything we have.

So often, we get caught up in the monotony of everyday life and forget to chase our hopes and dreams. Instead, we tell ourselves that we will start tomorrow, or next week, or when things slow down at work. But the truth is, there is never a perfect time to pursue our ambitions. Life is an adventure; if we are not careful, it can pass us by while waiting for the right moment. So instead of putting your dreams on hold, go out and chase them. Embrace the unknown. Follow your heart. And most importantly, do not wait. Because if you do, you might find that it is too late.

Don't Wait

How often have you said to yourself, "I'll do that tomorrow," or "I'll do it next week," and then never actually got around to doing it? We all do it; it is called procrastination. And while it might not seem like a big deal to put something off for a day or two, when you do it repeatedly, it can start to hold you back in life.

Think about everything you have been meaning to do but keep putting off. Maybe you want to start your own business, learn a new language, or finally take that dream vacation. Whatever it is, do not wait any longer.

Do not let procrastination steal your joy. Procrastination is often driven by fear or insecurity. It is also a form of self-sabotage. When we put off things we really want to do, we only cheat ourselves and others. Life is too short to wait for people who say they will do something but never actually follow through.

We only have one life to live, so we might as well make it a life full of adventure. Instead of waiting for others to take action, be the initiator yourself. Go out and explore the world with your friends and loved ones. Create memories that will last a lifetime. Life is too short to wait around.

Not everyone has the same dreams or goals as you, so spend your time with those who share your vision and appreciate you. There are many amazing things to discover, both about them and yourself. And what better way to bond with someone than by going on an adventure together, whether it is whitewater rafting down the Sunwapta River, snorkeling in the Bahamas, visiting museums in Paris, or going to Disneyworld?

Whatever you do, take the time to cherish those who are important to you. Do not just talk about how you want to spend time with those you care about; take the time and enjoy the quality time.

Do not put it off another day—who knows what amazing things you may discover about them, yourself, and the natural world?

Lake Time

Nature Is Healing

One of the things I enjoy on a beautiful warm summer day is spending it out on the lake, whether it is taking our boat out on Lake Pend Oreille or Priest Lake. They are both beautiful lakes with breathtaking scenery. It is always so peaceful and relaxing. I love to watch the eagles as they soar above or dive down to catch a fish, and I also love watching the mountain goats climb the rocks.

The water is clear, calm, refreshing, and inviting for a swim. Sometimes I throw out my fishing line to see if a fish will bite. It is fun watching them nibble on the worm. (Just a note, we catch and release.)

We always enjoy a picnic, barbecue, or a meal at a restaurant on the water. It does not matter if we are alone or have family or friends; spending time on the water seems to take away any stress or anxiety. I feel more connected to nature and myself when I am surrounded by its beauty. There is something about being in nature that is healing and calming. It is the fresh air and the sound of the water lapping against the shore. I am grateful for these moments that remind me of the power and beauty of nature.

Nature has a way of washing away the stress of daily life. Whether it is the sound of a babbling brook, the scent of a fresh bloom, or the sight of a beautiful sunset, nature has the power to heal. For some, the healing power of nature comes from spending time in the great outdoors—hiking through forests, wading in rivers, or sitting silently under the stars. For others, it may come from bringing nature indoors with houseplants, or filling their home with nature-inspired art. But whichever way you find it, there is no denying that there is something special about the healing power of nature.

Do Others Want to Be with You?

Do others want to be with you? Have you ever thought about this?

When you are around people, do they tend to want to stay or leave? This may be the first time you were ever asked this, but it affects your life. If people want to be around you, you are a positive influence in their life. You make them feel good and enjoy their time spent with you.

On the other hand, if people don't want to be around you, you might constantly be complaining or have a negative attitude toward life or others. You might not make them feel welcomed or comfortable, so they would rather spend their time elsewhere. It is essential to think about how you make others feel when they are around you, because it can either positively or negatively affect your relationships. If you want people to enjoy their time with you, focus on being positive and upbeat. People will be drawn to your infectious energy. Be the kind of person that others want to be around.

Spending time with friends is one of the best things in life. They bring joy, laughter, and fun into our lives. But what makes a devoted friend? Someone who is always there for you, no matter what. Someone who listens to you, helps you when you are struggling, and celebrates your successes with you. Someone who makes you feel good about yourself and inspires you to be the best you can be. That is what a loyal friend is. And that's why spending time with them is so important.

When we are surrounded by people who make us feel good about ourselves, we cannot help but feel happy, energized, and hopeful about life. You have found yourself a devoted friend. If not, it is time to make some new friends. Life is too short to waste time with people who do not make us feel good. Seek out those who listen, inspire, encourage, and make you feel happy.

A Quiet Repose

Chapter 9
Communication

9

Listen

L istening is such an important communication skill, yet often it is the number one thing we do not do. When we don't take the time to really listen, that is when there is miscommunication and misunder-standings. Listening is not just hearing the words being said but also how they are being told. Are we listening to the tone of voice? Are we taking in the entire story or showing that we value them and what they have to say?

Often, we only listen so that we can tell our own stories or share our own experiences or thoughts. But what if we took the time to really listen? To really hear what someone else is saying? We would be surprised at how much we can learn about a person. If we take the time to listen, we can learn about their hopes, dreams, fears, and passions. We can understand what makes them tick and what motivates them. We can learn about their families, their friends, and their experiences.

We would be inspired by their story or encouraged by their words. Perhaps we would see things from a different perspective. When we take the time to really listen, we open ourselves up to new possibilities and new ways of thinking. We might even find that our own story is a little bit more interesting when seen through someone else's eyes. So next time you are in a conversation, resist the urge to jump in with your own thoughts, and take a moment to truly listen to what the other person is saying. You might be surprised at what you discover.

It is also important to listen to our inner voice. This is the voice that communicates with our higher selves, and it can guide us to our most significant potential. However, we often ignore this voice in favor of outside noise and distractions. One way to tune into our inner voice is to spend time in nature. When surrounded by nature's beauty and simplicity, it is easier to quiet the mind and listen to our hearts. Nature communication is a powerful tool that can encourage us to be our best selves. We can learn to listen to our inner voice and connect with our highest purpose by spending time in nature. In doing so, we can lead more fulfilling and meaningful lives. We learn what we value!

Values

What are your values? Have you ever asked yourself this? Knowing our values and beliefs helps us in everyday life. Values are the things that are important to us. We all have values that guide our lives, even if we don't always stop to think about them; for example, integrity, honesty, communication, and kindness. They guide our actions and our decision making. They determine your priorities in life, at work, and at home. When you know what is important, it is easier to stay true to yourself. It also helps you make decisions that align with your values. For example, suppose one of your values is positivity; you might choose to surround yourself with people with a similar outlook on life. By living according to your values, you can create a rich and fulfilling life.

1. Make a values list. It is a great way to clarify what is important to you. Not sure where to start? Here are a few tips. First, consider what is important to you in life. For example, do you value family, work, adventure, or creativity? There are no wrong answers, so go with your gut. (It can be helpful to make a separate list for home and work. This can help you to see where there may be some misalignment between your two worlds.)

2. Take some time to define your values. What do these things mean to you? Why are they important? If one of your values is communication, you might resolve to be more open and honest in your relationships. If you value encouragement, you might try to be more supportive of others.

Once you have clarity on your values, it's time to implement them. So how can you start living by your values? What small steps can you take each day to move closer to a life aligned with who you are?

When we make decisions based on our values, we create a life rich with friends, meaning, and fulfillment.

Finding friends with whom we share common values is a great way to build lasting relationships. When we know our own values, it helps us to communicate better with others and identify those who may share similar beliefs. This can encourage positive interactions and discourage negative ones, making it easier to find fulfilling relationships. In addition, sharing values can be a fun way to bond with others and build a sense of community. Whether exploring new interests or just enjoying time together, friendships based on shared values can be some of the most rewarding relationships we experience. So, take the time to get clear on your values and start living them each day.

Go to my website for a bonus worksheet:
www.powerofartandnature.com.

Gain Clarity

At some point in our lives, we all face a fork in the road where we must decide: Do we stay on the path we have always known, or venture out into the unknown? This can be a scary moment because it feels like there is so much at stake. But what if I told you, you have everything you need to make the right choice? You are the only one who knows what you want in life. You are the only one who knows what you need to be happy. We can do many things to help us gain clarity in our lives. So how do you gain clarity? Stop listening to your fears and stop listening to the doubters.

Listen to your heart. Follow your intuition. Surround yourself with positive people and energy. This can be done by spending time with loved ones, being around friends, or participating in activities that make us happy.

Finally, and most importantly, be true to yourself. When you do this, you will realize that you are responsible for your actions and capable of anything you set your mind to.

Another way to gain clarity is to spend time in nature. Nature has a way of washing away all the negativity in our lives and leaving us feeling refreshed and rejuvenated. Additionally, connecting with nature can help us tap into our creative side, which can be extremely helpful when solving problems or producing innovative ideas. Finally, prayer and meditation are excellent ways to calm the mind. Taking even just a few minutes out of each day to pray or meditate can make an enormous difference in our ability to gain clarity.

Express

Expressing your dreams and goals is a powerful way to implement them. It makes them seem more real and encourages you to take positive steps to make them happen. When you communicate your dreams with those you trust, it also allows you to get feedback and support that can help turn your dreams into reality. If you cannot find someone to talk to, try writing your goals down and then spending time in nature. Expressing your dreams is a step toward making them come true. So go ahead and speak them today!

Art and nature have always been a passion of mine. When I spend time in nature, it makes me feel more creative. It is a form of self-expression that allows me to be creative and have fun. I enjoy art because it's a way to express my feelings, thoughts, and dreams. Art is also a way to communicate, encourage, and inspire others. The power of art is in its ability to share our dreams and goals in a way that inspires us to take action. The power of nature is its ability to give us the creativity we need to express our dreams and goals. Communication connects us with others who can encourage and support us as we work toward making our dreams come true. The power of encouragement is its ability to give us the motivation to keep going when things get tough. The power of inspiration is its ability to show us what is possible and remind us why we are pursuing our dreams in the first place. When we combine all these powers together, we have the potential to create something truly magical.

Kindness and Calmness

We live in a world where the power of communication is ever-increasing. With the advent of social media, we can now reach out to anyone, anywhere in the world. However, with this great power comes great responsibility. Let us use our words to encourage and inspire others rather than to tear them down. When we communicate with kindness and calmness, we set an example for others to follow.

We all know the feeling of being in the middle of an intense argument. The adrenaline is pumping, the heart is racing, and the words start flying. Yet, it can be challenging in those moments to remember that there is more power in kindness and calmness than in yelling and fighting.

But what if we could view arguments as an opportunity to practice the power of communication, to truly listen to what the other person is saying, and to respond with gentleness and poise? Instead of getting wrapped up in our egos, we could see arguments as an opportunity to learn and grow.

When we communicate with kindness and calmness, we open the possibility for real understanding and connection. We might not always agree, but we can at least walk away feeling respected and heard. So next time you find yourself in the middle of a disagreement, remember the power of communication. Let's encourage each other to speak with kindness and calmness.

Don't Just Talk; Act

We all know the saying that "actions speak louder than words." But how often do we live by those words? Every day, we encounter people who talk a big game but never actually follow through. They make grandiose plans and promises but never take any real action to make them happen. This can be incredibly frustrating, especially when we see others wasting their time with empty talk instead of taking productive steps forward.

Fortunately, we do not have to let this negative behavior drag us down. Instead, we can choose to lead by example and show others that it is possible to turn our dreams into reality. Every time we act toward our goals, we send a powerful message to those around us. We are showing them that it is possible to turn talk into action and that real change is possible if we are brave enough to go after what we want.

So be brave and don't just talk; act. That is how our world moves forward. When people take inspired action and communicate their ideas with others, things get done! So next time you find yourself in a group of people talking about what should be done, ask yourself if you are part of the problem or part of the solution, and then take action accordingly. The world needs more doers!

The Hunter

Chapter 10
Lifestyle

10

What's Missing?

D
o you ever feel like something is missing from your life? Maybe you can't put your finger on it, but you know something is not quite right. If you are feeling this way, you are not alone. Many people go through life searching for something they cannot quite identify. It might be a sense of security, happiness, or even just a sense of fulfillment. Whatever it is, we all have a void we are trying to fill.

For some people, the answer is finding a career or hobby they are passionate about. This can give them a sense of purpose and make them feel like they are doing something worthwhile with their time. Others might start a family or get involved in their community to feel more connected to the world around them. And still, others might choose to travel and explore new places to broaden their horizons and see the world from a new perspective.

You know that feeling when you are stuck in a rut, going through the motions daily with no end in sight? Getting caught up in the mundane can be easy, and you forget what it feels like to truly live. But there's hope! By making a few slight changes in your daily routine, you can learn to embrace a lifestyle that is fun and full of adventure. It might sound daunting at first, but trust me, it is worth it! Here are a few things you can do to get started:

- Make time for hobbies and interests that you are passionate about. Whether painting, hiking, or rock climbing, find an activity that brings you joy and stick with it.

- Get out of your comfort zone. Challenging yourself is a terrific way to learn new things and build confidence. Plus, it is just plain fun!

- Be social. Spend time with friends and family, go out on dates, or join a club or sports team. The people in your life can make all the difference.

- Live in the present. One of the best ways to enjoy life is to focus on the here and now instead of worrying about what tomorrow might bring. Relax and take it one day at a time.

Committing to living a more fulfilling life may seem like a lot of work, but trust me, it is worth it. So, what are you waiting for? Get out there and start living!

Living vs. Being

Have you ever googled living vs. being? What is interesting is that no one seems to agree on a definition. Some say that living is breathing, eating, and sleeping, while being alive is living at a higher level of consciousness and achieving your dreams. The second definition says the opposite. It is interesting how two different people can have such different opinions.

There is no single right or wrong answer regarding living vs. being. It is all a matter of perspective. So, what are your thoughts on this topic? Do you agree with one definition more than the other? Or do you have your own unique opinion?

I have always thought of "being" as going through the motions day by day, existing but not really thriving. Too often, we allow others to control our lives and dictate our choices. So, we follow the path they have laid out for us instead of striking out on our own. Life is meant to be enjoyed, not just endured. But what if this isn't the life we were meant to live? What if we are meant to be doing something different? Everyone has their own unique path to follow, and that is what makes life so interesting.

Living is about being creative, taking risks, and encouraging others to do the same. It is about living life on your own terms, pursuing your passions and dreams and doing what makes you happy, while enjoying life's simple things. It is about finding a lifestyle you want and making the most of every moment. So, ask yourself: Are you living or just existing?

It is time to take control of our lives and start living the way we want. So, ask yourself: Are you living, or are you just being? The choice is yours. Just remember to live life to the fullest and enjoy the journey!

What Makes You Happy?

What is happiness? What makes you happy? It is different for everyone. Some people find joy in nature, while others find it in a more creative outlet. What makes you happy? Maybe it's encouraging others or simply enjoying a good lifestyle. Whatever it is, let us explore happiness and what it means to different people.

For some, happiness comes from spending time outdoors in nature. They might find joy in hiking through the woods or relaxing by a river. The fresh air and beauty of nature can be very rejuvenating. Others might find happiness in more creative outlets, such as painting, writing, or playing music. This can be a wonderful way to express yourself and connect with your inner thoughts and feelings.

What makes you happy? What is happiness to you? Take some time to think about it and explore what brings a smile to your face. Again, happiness is different for everyone.

What brings happiness into my life? What things make me feel whole, complete, and at peace with myself? Many things make me happy. I enjoy working in the studio creating wall sculptures, painting, teaching, or spending the day in nature. Being around family is one of the things I enjoy most. We always have so much fun, whether shopping, going to a movie, boating, exploring new areas side by side, or just spending time making a meal together.

The power of nature never fails to amaze me. The beauty of a sunset, the colors of a rainbow, or the simple act of watching a bird build its nest can fill me with joy. Art is another passion of mine that brings happiness into my life. The creative process is therapeutic and allows me to express myself uniquely. I also enjoy encouraging others to explore their creativity. Seeing someone discover their own artistic talents and develop a love for art is so fulfilling.

Happiness is a lifestyle for me. I am constantly looking for ways to bring more joy into my life and surround myself with positive people and experiences. When I am happy, I dream of doing even more!

Dream

A dream is an act of imagination. It is a mental activity that includes images, sounds, and feelings. Dreams may be public (communal) or private (personal), but they are invariably dreamt in the first person. A dream can be defined as a visionary psychic revelation or natural vision that comes to us. At the same time, we are asleep, or it may be an inspiration, daydream, or waking dream. Dreams are often surreal, fantastic, weird, nonsensical, and dreamlike. The stuff of dreams is not bound by the laws of physics or realism.

I have always been fascinated by dreams and what they mean. To me, dreams are a way to access our subconscious mind and tap into our creativity. I believe that everyone can dream and that dreams are a window into our souls.

Dreams encourage us to think outside the box and to view the world differently. They inspire us to be creative and to see things from a different perspective. We can fly, explore distant worlds, or meet long-lost friends. We are free to do anything we can imagine for a few hours. Dreams can also be a way to work through issues we are facing in our lives. They can also help us better understand our nature, goals, and desires.

I believe that dreams are an essential part of who we are and that they should be embraced as part of our lifestyle. Dreams help us to grow and evolve as individuals. They challenge us to think differently and to view the world in a new light. Dreams can be a source of immense joy and fulfillment or encourage us to be more creative in our waking lives.

Dreams are one of the most fascinating and mysterious aspects of our lives. In the morning, we may not remember our dreams clearly, but they can still have a powerful impact on us. Dreams have been studied for centuries, and there is still much we do not understand about them. However, one thing is clear: Dreams are a uniquely human experience that can inspire us, challenge us, and even change our lives.

Live the Lifestyle You Dream Of

Do you ever feel like you are not living the life you want? Are you stuck in a job you do not like or living in a place you don't want to be? It is easy to get caught up in the mundane day-to-day and forget our dreams. But it is important to remember that we are the ones who create our own lives. We are the ones who make the choices that determine our lifestyle. So, if you are not happy with your current situation, make a change. Life is too short to settle for anything less than your dream life.

Don't let your fears hold you back. Get out there and live the life you have always wanted to live. Do the things you love and make new memories. Appreciate the beauty of nature and the creativity of humankind. Encourage others to chase their dreams, and be an inspiration for them. Live your life with intention and make every day count. You only have one life to live, so make it matter!

Dreams and goals are what keep life interesting. They give us something to strive for and something to look forward to. However, it is important to remember that our dreams and goals will likely change over time. That is not necessarily a bad thing; change can be good. It can mean that we're evolving and growing as individuals.

For me, I am living the life I want. No, it is not perfect, but I am living right where I want to live, doing what I want to do, spending time with those I want to spend time with, and enjoying life. I chose a positive life filled with God, nature, inspiration, and fun. And that is what I am going to continue to choose every day. You only have one life to live, so make it count! Live the lifestyle you dream of! You deserve it!

Final Touches

Art and Nature Together

The power of art is often underestimated. Many people see art as a way to kill time or express themselves, but it can be much more. Art has the power to inspire change, teach us about unfamiliar cultures, and encourage us to see the world in new ways. It can even be used as a form of healing. Nature is one of the most common inspirations for artists. A beautiful sunset over a majestic mountain or the bends in a river, can be captured in a painting or sculpture. By looking at art, we can appreciate the power and beauty of nature, even if we have never seen it firsthand. Art can also be used to promote a lifestyle change.

Everything from fashion to architecture is influenced by art. By seeing how other people live, we can be inspired to make changes in our own lives. Whether it encourages us to travel, try new foods, or simply see the world in a new light, art has the power to change lives.

There is something about nature that has the power to heal. Maybe it's the fresh air, the calming sounds of the waves, or the warm sun on your skin. Whatever it is, time in nature has been shown to have a variety of benefits for both our physical and mental health. And as more of us spend time indoors, it is more important than ever to find ways to connect with the natural world. One way to do this is to incorporate elements of nature into your daily life. For example, you could go for a walk in the park, grow some plants on your balcony, or decorate your home with nature-inspired artwork. By doing so, you can enjoy the healing power of nature every day.

There is something special about the power of art and nature together. They are healing and inspiring, and when you add them both to your life, you can create the lifestyle of your dreams. Art can move us emotionally, connect us with our innermost thoughts and feelings, and encourage us to express ourselves in new and creative ways. On the other hand, nature has the power to soothe and relax us, provide a sense of peace and calm, and remind us of the beauty of the world around us. When we combine these two powerful forces, we can create a lifestyle that is both meaningful and fulfilling. We can find inspiration in the simplest things and use creativity to make our dreams a reality. So, if you are looking for a way to add more beauty and joy to your life, consider adding art and nature together. You may be surprised at just how powerful they are.

I am so grateful that you took the time to read my book, and I truly hope that it has inspired you in some way. Spending time in nature and discovering your creative side can be such a rewarding experience. It is my sincerest hope that my story, and the golden nuggets I shared, touched your soul and that you will take away something positive from it. Remember to always be thankful for what you have, do your best each day, and be an inspiration to others.

Go to my website for a bonus worksheet:
www.powerofartandnature.com.

MitzkaFineArts, Copper Mountain

Made in the USA
Las Vegas, NV
21 October 2022